Treasure Trove of Memories

**Essays from an Award-Winning
Alzheimer's Blog**

earlyonset.blogspot.com

By

L. S. Fisher

MoZark

www.MozarkPress.com

Published by Mozark Press, www.Mozarkpress.com
PO Box 1746, Sedalia, MO 65302

Cover Photo: "Treasure Trove" by L.S. Fisher

Acknowledgement: Cover design and book layout by H.D. Ream

DISCLAIMER: *Statements or opinions expressed in the stories and articles of this publication are those of the author and do not necessarily represent the views or positions of any person or entity associated with publication of the book or the Alzheimer's Association.*

ISBN: 978-0-9903270-7-3

Dedication

Early Onset Alzheimer's Blog is dedicated to Jimmy D. Fisher and to all whose lives have been disrupted by a debilitating disease and to their families.

Other Titles by L. S. Fisher

Alzheimer's Anthology of
Unconditional Love

Early Onset Blog
Essays from an Online Journal
(Ozark Writers League 2010 Book of the Year)

Early Onset Blog
The Friendship Connection and Other Essays

Early Onset Alzheimer's
Encourage, Inspire, and Inform

Early Onset Alzheimer's
My Recollections, Our Memories

Focus on the Positive

Garden of Hope

The Broken Road

At the End of the Day

The Heart Remembers

Available at www.lsfisher.com

Table of Contents

Introduction

Scientifically, we store our memories in our brains, but intuitively, we store our memories in our hearts. The saddest part of dementia is that memories are erased from the brain. The first to go are the short-term memories.

As we travel through our lives, we store up a treasure trove of memories. We can find physical reminders in the form of a souvenir from a vacation, a photo of a loved one, videos, a hand-written letter, a greeting card, or a thousand other whispers from days gone by.

Old photographs are snippets of time we store as treasures of the heart. They are reminders of who we once were.

Our brains have stored up millions of "snapshots" from different times in our lives. Photos can help us retrieve memories so deep-seated that we may have never thought of them again.

One day I came home from work and the caregiver I hired to stay with Jim said, "He showed me your daughter's wedding photo! He said 'Stacey's wedding.'"

I had to smile that he had shared the memory with her. "Well," I said. "That is our son's wedding photo, but our daughter-in-law is Stacey."

When Jim was in the nursing home, he had some small photo albums with photos of family. Sometimes he would surprise visitors by pointing at a photo and saying, "Bob and Barb." He seldom spoke, and it was reassuring that some of his precious long-term memories were triggered by photographs.

The hundreds of photos and mementos I saved will connect me to my past. The photos I take now will link my present to my future. My treasure trove overflows with memories and reminds me that I've always been a link in a huge circle of love.

~ Linda Fisher

Choices, Chance, and Monopoly

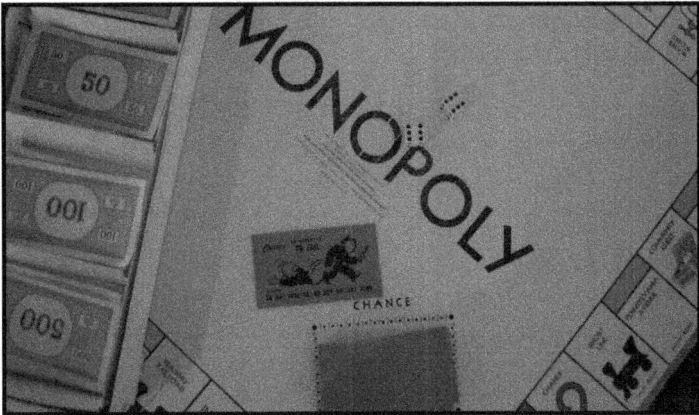

A few weeks ago, my grandson went to the closet where we keep our games and came out with a vintage Monopoly game. I hadn't played the game since I was a kid and sure didn't remember anything about it or the rules.

My grandson gave "money" to Harold and me and the game began. It turned out to be a game of choices and chance. The roll of the dice could give you a chance to purchase properties, pay rent or taxes, draw a "chance" or "community chest" card, or maybe "go to jail." It didn't take long for me to find out what the expression, "do not pass go," meant.

My son, who was watching us play, noticed something rather peculiar. "Mom, you are being so cautious about what you spend, and Harold is buying without a second thought. That's totally the opposite of how you are in real life." I had to agree.

Spending habits aside, the game made me think about how each of us has a monopoly on our own destiny. Have you ever stopped to think how much your life would be affected if you had made one major choice differently than you did? Or what if that lucky break hadn't come your way?

Chance can put us in dangerous situations. Decisions can lessen the danger or increase it. How often have you heard someone say, "If that had happened to me, I would have... (blah, blah, blah)." One thing I've learned in life, no person will ever know what he would do in someone else's situation. I don't have a clue *why* they react the way they do, because I have not lived the same life.

In my own life, I met Jim by chance, chose to marry him, and chose to work at it. Dementia cut his life short by chance, and I chose to become an Alzheimer's volunteer, which brought about a major change in my life. I've gone places I would have never gone, had experiences I would not have had, and found friends I would have never met.

Who we are and what we've become is a conglomeration of choice and chance. Sometimes, we might not even distinguish the difference. Have you ever noticed how many of us go to college and never work in the field we studied? Sometimes, that's choice and sometimes it's chance. Maybe we couldn't find that special job we wanted. The winds of chance did not blow in our direction. Sometimes, we just grow older and decide that wasn't the career path for us.

At one time, I wanted to be a teacher. Then, I wanted to be a journalist. What really happened was I became a mom and stayed home with the kids while they were little. My first real job after returning to college was in subscriptions at a coonhound magazine. Believe me, I never saw that coming!

After that company moved out of town, I, by chance, was selected to interview for a job on a computer. You have to realize that I had never seen a computer, much less used one. I chose to believe that it was something I always wanted to experience. That choice changed our family's economic situation. Up until then, we had spent several years living frugally and still barely getting by.

Nine years after Jim passed away, I chose to remarry. So, here I am, in this house, in this room, at this table, working on this PC because of a lifetime of choices and by chance. It's a scary thought that my destiny would have changed if I had made one different decision along the way. Yes, I have a monopoly on my life. No one else will ever have the exact experiences or make the same decisions I have made.

On the other hand, I've always had a feeling that the choices and chances I took were meant to be. I seriously doubt that I've always made the wisest or even the most logical choice. My decisions have been good, bad, and ugly, and yet somehow, in the end, it worked out.

I believe I've often been "nudged" along the right path. *My* path.

The Fierce Urgency of Now

Yesterday, I watched the Kansas City Chiefs play the Steelers in a playoff game. Any year the Chiefs made the playoffs, we fans were hopeful the Chiefs would make it to the Super Bowl. We always hoped we wouldn't be disappointed—again.

During commercial breaks, I watched other fans' reactions online. About the time I realized the Chiefs were going to fall to the curse of their playoff games, a photo of a youthful Jim popped up on my Facebook newsfeed.

Jim was the sole reason that I became a Chiefs fan. Through winning seasons and losing seasons, he was steadfast in his loyalty. During the early years of our marriage, Monday night football was opposite the movie of the week. With one TV set, I never watched a single movie during football season.

Although, it seemed magical that Jim's photo appeared on my phone just as I was thinking of him, I scrolled past other old family photos. Jim's cousin Debbie had decided to make an online album of old family photos, and I assumed she had posted the photo.

I downloaded the photo and added it to my own online album of Jim's pictures.

"Can I steal this for the Fisher album?" she asked.

"I just stole it myself. That's where I thought it was," I replied.

It didn't take me long to figure out that my nephew John had posted it.

Seeing Jim's photo put a lot of perspective in my outlook, and reminded me of the real urgency of now. When he was diagnosed with dementia of the Alzheimer's type, my goal became to do anything possible to change the outcome.

The urgency to do something, rather than patiently wait for the inevitable, was part of my nature. I trolled the internet looking for anything to stave off a degenerative, fatal disease. I tried to get Jim enrolled in drug trials. He was turned down for one trial because he was too young and for another because he had lost the ability to communicate.

I began to go to the Alzheimer's forum to advocate for more research dollars. I saw the urgency to find a cure in the eyes of other caregivers, and my heart hurt for them. I felt their pain and knew the disappointment of hearing a doctor say, "Even if they find a cure, the disease is so far advanced that it's too late for him."

As the years went by and the disease won, I continued my advocacy, as have many others who lost loved ones. We all share the same hopes and dreams—a cure for Alzheimer's.

I recently read the "I Have a Dream" speech Martin Luther King, Jr., delivered at the Lincoln Memorial in 1963. Although his speech was loaded with quotable sentences, one phrase caught and held my attention. King spoke of "the fierce urgency of now."

Many of us won't step out of our comfort zone to fight for our cause with the conviction of Martin Luther King, Jr. Most of us anonymously fight our fight. Some of the rich and famous meet the challenge as they or their loved ones discover Alzheimer's when it strikes close to home.

Just this week, I learned that Marty Schottenheimer, the former head coach of the Kansas City Chiefs, has Alzheimer's. This too, helps me put the Chiefs loss into its proper perspective. Next season, the Chiefs have a new start and a chance to redeem themselves.

As far as Alzheimer's, there are no second chances. With more people dying each day that passes without a cure, we have the "fierce urgency of now" to end Alzheimer's.

Grace under Fire

I had such a busy week that when Saturday rolled around, I plopped on the couch and turned on the TV. I began watching the twenty hours or so of the European Figure Skating championships recorded on the DVR. This gluttonous devouring reiterated my opinion that a figure skating competition is the epitome of grace under fire.

Countries sent only their top skaters to the competition, but most knew they were not in medal contention. Some found victory by participating in the competition, while others were only satisfied with one of the top three slots.

Some of the performances were so nearly perfect that a small bobble made the difference between earning a coveted medal, or going home empty handed. It was easy to show grace when everything went according to plan, but those that truly showed their spirit were the ones who fell, jumped back up, and continued doing their very best.

The expert commentators knew immediately when someone faltered. The skater's foot touched too soon, they didn't quite complete a rotation, or pairs were not in unison. Skaters made "silly mistakes" when they completed difficult jumps and then stumbled on an easy element.

It made me think about being a caregiver. I could often handle the messy and difficult parts of caregiving, but might fall apart over a broken nail. Why was that? I believe that I forced myself to meet the tough challenges with acceptance and a sense of loving duty.

Oh, but when it came to the simple setbacks, I stumbled.

I can't think of many things that rival the beauty of figure skating. Each move is choreographed to carefully selected music. Music helps set the tone whether figure skating or drudging through a day that seems almost too much to tolerate.

During my time as a caregiver, I remember days when I was up before daylight to work ten hours and then went by the nursing home in the evening to feed and bathe Jim. It was unusual for me to make it to bed before midnight.

In the journal I kept while Jim was in the nursing home, I would tell about my day and often say, "I am so tired." Thinking back, that's what I remember the most—being tired. Exhausted. Like I was running on empty.

Being chronically tired often means that grace goes by the wayside. To this day, being tired makes me cranky and more than a bit whiney.

Caregiving, like figure skating, greatly improves with practice. When we put ourselves out there, so to speak, we open ourselves up for criticism or derision. Caregiving is like figure skating in that sense. The critics will sit back and watch someone else struggle and pontify how it could have been done better or more efficiently. When a caregiver provides caregiving with love and grace, it just doesn't get any better.

Taking care of a loved one is much like walking through fire. It hurts like hell, but unless you keep on moving, you're going to be charred beyond recognition.

None of us makes it through life without faltering. The best we can hope for is to demonstrate grace under fire. No one gets a medal for being the best caregiver in the world. Our reward comes from being the best caregiver *we* can be.

Treasure Trove of Memories

Yesterday I dove into the treasure trove of memories stored in the basement of the house that Jim built. One large box had been water damaged from a drippy faucet, and I'd never had the heart to go through the hodgepodge inside that pitiful box until yesterday.

I tossed old Memory Walk memos, agendas, brochures, and various papers from the years I coordinated the Sedalia Walk. I found two warped notebooks and sifted through the memories. One had photos front and back in the notebook's protective cover sleeve. The photo on the front was ruined, but when I flipped the book over, I saw a perfectly preserved photo from a "Night to Remember Dance."

My eyes blurred as I looked at a photo of Ted Distler and me dancing. Ted and I were friendly rivals.

He coordinated the Jefferson City walk, and we always tried to out-do each other. The rivalry only spurred each of us to do our best. I attended his chicken dinner and auction, and he supported our dance and auction. It seemed there was always a gooseberry pie at both events and the winner was either him or me. Those pies were never cheap!

Another role Ted and I shared was that of caregiver. His lovely wife Norma was the center of his world and, is often the case, the disease took a terrible toll on both of them.

To say that Ted was my friend is an understatement. He was more like family. We would lose touch for a few months, but he'd call me or I would call him. Then, one day I received a call from the Alzheimer's Association letting me know that Ted had passed away. Norma soon joined him.

Next, I pulled out a box of thank you notes. I opened the box and discovered a stack of photos. The one on top was a smiling Jim wearing a "Colby's Grandpa" hat and holding our oldest grandson. I leafed through the photos—Jim in Estes Park and at an early Memory Walk.

I carried items upstairs, and when I went back down, I saw a red crate filled with photos that never made it to the photo albums. I opened an envelope and the first photo I saw was Jim playing his guitar. Easter photos taken two decades ago brought an avalanche of memories.

I found memories scattered in places they shouldn't be. Why had I thrown this batch of pictures in a crate instead of putting them away in photo boxes or albums?

My guess is that since most of these were taken around the time that life made a left turn, more pressing matters took priority.

This morning, I began the long organizational process by throwing away the extra envelopes and negatives. Next, I will try to put the envelopes in chronological order. I plan to throw away the out-of-focus photos and pictures of people I don't know, or care to know, including people on stage in Branson.

Finding the old photos felt like finding a hidden treasure. I saw the innocent faces of children who are now adults with kids of their own. I saw the smiles of beloved family members who are long gone and felt the warm breath of their spirits. The real treasure trove, I realized, was the reminder that I've always been a link in a huge circle of love.

You Know What I Hate?

It seems that people are getting bolder and nastier in their communications. I'm not much of a hater, but when I thought about it, there were a few things at the top of my list.

I hate consecutive months with dates that fall on the same day of the week. Let me explain. My hairdresser called me at work one day wondering why I hadn't shown up for my appointment. "I don't have it on my calendar," I said. Flipped the calendar and sure enough there it was—same day of the week, same date, different month.

This calendar issue has caused me grief in the past and came close to causing me grief this week. I've been planning to go to a conference Friday and Saturday. It was on the wall calendar for February 3-4, but while setting up a conference call for next month, I saw the conference on my electronic calendar for March 3-4. Holy moly, sure glad I didn't drive to Jefferson City an entire month early.

I hate the paint MO-Dot uses on the roads. It doesn't take long for the lines to fade away and I don't have confidence that I'm inside my lane. This is especially dicey driving through town in the rain with streetlights and car lights glaring off the pavement. The older I get, the harder it is to see the lines. I want glow in the dark paint on our highways like the Netherlands has. Is that too much to ask?

I hate tax time. It isn't even so much paying the taxes as it is gathering all the papers together, bringing everything up to date in Quicken, and then putting the info on TurboTax. Everything is complicated, and it makes my head hurt. I'd so much rather be doing something else. Much, much rather, be doing just about anything else.

I hate junk mail and junk email. Try as I might, I can't get rid of those two. I unsubscribe, report as spam, block, grit my teeth, and swear. Nothing helps. Right up there with junk email is email that requires me to complete a task when I'd rather be relaxing. It's easy to be sucked into a project that's taking much more of my time than is warranted.

I hate debilitating disease especially Alzheimer's. And cancer. And heart disease. And diabetes. And anything that makes a person suffer. I hate to watch someone dying. I wish we could live long, healthy lives, and when it was our time, we'd leap on that chariot of fire and ascend into heaven in a blaze of glory.

I hate homelessness. Every time I go to D.C. for the Alzheimer's forum, I see dozens of the 11,623 homeless people that live in that city. No one should have to curl up on a park bench or huddle in a doorway on a cold winter's night. One year, I was sitting in the lobby of a five-star D.C. hotel when this lady walked inside. She wore a long flowing animal print dress, but I noticed she wasn't wearing a bra.

A hotel worker rushed out from behind the desk and confronted her. "You have to leave or I'll call the police," he told her.

"Please don't call the police. I don't have any place to stay and it's cold outside," she replied in a soft voice.

"There's a homeless shelter a couple of blocks from here," he said. Then, he showed her the door on a cold winter's night, and she went on her way.

I hate that we are never going to have world peace. It is impossible in a world where power means more than people, and religion means more than faith, and we focus on our differences rather than our commonalities.

I hate Cajun toast. The identical twin look of Cajun and cinnamon seasonings caused me to serve my granddaughter Cajun toast when she was little. To be sure, it had some sugar in it, but it was still nasty. Earlier this week I went to sprinkle cinnamon sugar on my toast and I reached for the Rubbermaid mini container where I keep it. Well, I also keep cinnamon creamer in an identical container, but caught myself. I reached into the cabinet and pulled out another container thinking this was surely the right one. The smell was a clue that my husband used one of the minis for something that smelled suspiciously like Cajun seasoning. Finally, third time was a charm.

Yes, there are a few things I hate in this world, but many, many more that I love.

Seven Types of Love

When February 14 rolls around, hearts and minds everywhere focus on love. Some look forward to the day with unbridled anticipation, while others feel only trepidation. During our lifetimes, most of us will experience both feelings depending on how life is going at that moment.

Love can be enduring, or elusive. It can be the center of our dreams, or the crux of our nightmares. Love can bring us to the mountaintop or plunge us into the deepest, darkest valley.

Valentine's Day celebrates all kinds of love. According to the ancient Greeks, there are seven different types of love. I'm not sure that all the emotions we humans call "love" can be narrowed down to seven categories, but I suppose it's a start.

1. *Eros*, or erotic love, represents the physical body. This type of love has all the passion and desire to fuel a romance. It is because of *Eros* love that Cupid wears a blindfold.

2. *Philia*, or affectionate love, is the love we feel for our friends who have our backs through the bad times in our lives. These trusted friends provide the chocolate cake when our romantic love hits rock bottom.
3. *Storge* is familial love. *Storge* is the type of love we feel for our parents and children. It can also be the fondness we have toward childhood friends where the relationship is built on familiarity and acceptance.
4. The playful love of *ludus* is found during the early stages of falling in love. That's when just seeing the interest of our affections can set our hearts all aflutter. *Ludus* can also describe the relationship of friends who enjoy hanging out with each other.
5. *Pragma* is enduring or practical love. This kind of love is found in married couples who have made the effort to maintain their relationship through compromise, patience, and tolerance. It can also be found in couples who stay together for political, social, or other practical reasons.
6. *Philautia* is self-love. In this sense, it is a good thing! In order to truly love someone else, it is necessary to first love yourself. *Philautia* is unhealthy when a person places himself before others.
7. *Agape* is the purest love. It is selfless love free of expectations that accepts and forgives. *Agape* is unconditional love.

We all understand that in a romantic relationship, we give our hearts, and we expect that love to be reciprocated. Since Cupid is blindfolded, sometimes love is blind. We focus only on the good qualities and overlook the irritating ones. Whether we survive the unique personality traits that makes up every human being on earth depends on how much effort we put into keeping the love alive.

When we look at the different kinds of love, it is easy to see that *agape*, or unconditional love, is the type of love that caregivers have for their loved ones with dementia. When Jim developed dementia, my love for him became multidimensional and included both *pragma* and *storge*. I often likened my love for Jim to that of a mother for her child. More importantly, I don't believe that the love of a caregiver fits neatly into some Greek or psychologist's category.

Each of us is a unique individual with an individual capacity for love. Not even a scientist can accurately measure the love one person has for another.

A lot of hearts given on Valentine's Day are not worth the paper they are printed on. The real value of a Valentine's heart is determined by how we treat the ones we love the other 364 days of the year and throughout the years of a lifetime.

Sources:

https://lonerwolf.com/different-types-of-love/
https://www.psychologytoday.com/blog/hide-and-seek/201606/the-7-types-love

Alzheimer's Caregiving
A Voice of Experience

At the end of January, my friend and mentor, Penny Braun passed away. Penny was my first contact with the Alzheimer's Association. When Jim first developed dementia symptoms, I called the Mid-Missouri Chapter, located in Columbia. The executive director, Penny, answered the phone.

"I don't know if I should be calling you because my husband has memory problems but has not been diagnosed with Alzheimer's," I said.

"You called the right place," Penny assured me. "We have information that will help you, and you can call us anytime." And I did.

Penny brought her beloved German shepherd, Victoria, with her when she came to the 1998 Sedalia Memory Walk. Penny wasn't in any of the photos because she took them, but Victoria posed with the small group that walked that day.

In 2001, Penny asked me to go to the Alzheimer's forum.

"We're going to ask for a billion dollars," she told me. "Maureen Reagan set that goal when she was on the national Alzheimer's board."

"I can do that," I said with much more confidence than I felt. I had no concept of what a billion dollars looked like. Of course, the research funding was only a small fraction of that billion-dollar goal.

Penny and I shared a room on my first trip to Washington, D.C. We arrived late and when we tried to check in, the clerk clicked the keyboard on the computer, frowned and clicked some more.

"I don't have a reservation for you," he said, "and we're booked solid."

"We do have a reservation," Penny said firmly, "I have the paperwork here." Penny dug in her purse for the reservation. When she couldn't find it, she turned on the charm. "We're exhausted, and surely you can find one room we can have. Please, check with your manager and see if you can find a room for this old lady."

When he left to check, she turned to me and said, "They always save one room in case the president or some important person needs a room. Oh, here it is!" She jubilantly pulled out the reservation, gave it a glance, and stuffed it back into her purse. "It begins tomorrow night," she said in a stage whisper. About that time, the clerk returned all smiles, and handed us the keys to a beautiful suite. Mission accomplished.

After Penny retired from the Alzheimer's Association to care for her husband, I saw her only occasionally. She was at the Alzheimer's roast last spring. She, of course, gave me a big hug and asked how I was doing. "Have you read my book?" she asked.

When I admitted I hadn't, she pulled a copy of *Alzheimer's Caregiving: A Voice of Experience* out of her purse and handed it to me. Penny knew the heartbreak of Alzheimer's because her mother had the disease. Her family connection compelled her to open the office in Columbia, first as a volunteer. She later became the chapter's first executive director.

Penny's book has several examples of situations and solutions to problems that "might work." She was smart enough to know that the same solutions don't work for every person, nor do the same solutions always work for the same person.

I had to smile when I got to the "Three Right Answers." She wrote, "As the disease progresses, three answers to problems seem inevitably right. The first two are music and ice cream." The final right answer is the smile. "Use it warmly and often."

Rest in peace, my friend. You left a legacy of hugs, smiles, and a caring heart.

Blowin' in the Wind

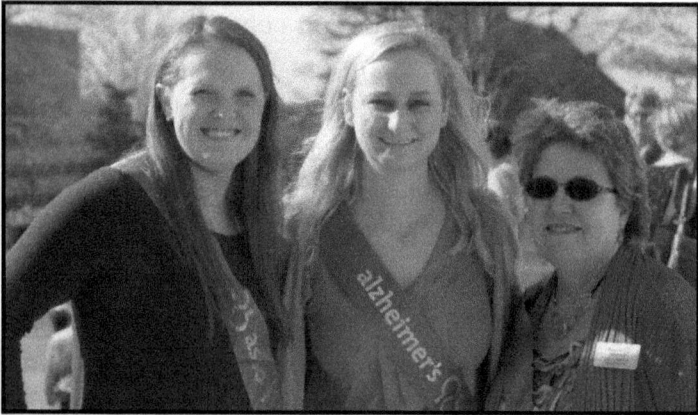

As usual, I was running late for an appointment this morning. As I turned onto the highway, I noticed my *Sedalia Democrat* had been delivered to my paper box. Deciding I could be on time if I didn't waste the couple of minutes to pick up the paper, I left it.

After my appointment, I made my usual stop at Walmart. As I pushed my cart into the parking lot, I had to battle the wind to keep the cart going forward instead of sideways. Talk about a strong wind! The wind buffeted my car on the way home, and I parked at the end of the driveway to get my paper and mail. The paper was gone. I looked around and found it lying in the ditch.

After I retrieved the paper, I grabbed a stack of mail out of the mailbox. The wind ripped a few pieces out of my hands and whimsically scattered them into the aforementioned ditch. Have you ever chased paper that a gust of wind takes out of your reach time after time?

The Bob Dylan song "Blowin' in the Wind" came to mind. Bits and pieces of the lyrics teased my memory. I remembered unanswered questions about manhood, white doves, cannon balls, mountains washing to the sea, and pretending not to notice freedom lost.

The most haunting line in Dylan's song is about too many people dying. Every year 700,000 people die from Alzheimer's, and so far, we haven't been able to do one thing to stop it. Not one single thing!

Alzheimer's disease is the sixth leading cause of death in the United States. Approximately 5.4 million people are living, and dying, with the disease. Around 200,000 people younger than age 65 have Alzheimer's. Many are much, much younger.

Each year I join other advocates nationally to advocate for more research funds. In our packets, we have information that compares research funds for Alzheimer's to the amount allocated to fight other diseases. This dedication to fighting diseases has paid big dividends. At one time, a diagnosis of HIV/AIDS was a death sentence. Research has played a huge role in finding effective treatments for cancer and heart disease.

Lately, two promising drug therapies failed during drug trials. When these treatments failed, we were disappointed, but we haven't given up.

Some of the brightest minds are working diligently to cure this incurable disease. In the meantime, it is important that caregivers and persons with dementia have the care and support they need to live life to the fullest. Those on the front lines need respite, home and community based support, family support, and a reason to hope. They need to know that we have their backs.

I was at the Missouri State Capitol on Memory Day advocating for respite funds. The Missouri state budget has been slashed, including a big reduction in the $450,000 service grants that our friends, neighbors, and families rely on for respite. This is a case of saving pennies and costing dollars. Respite helps keep persons with Alzheimer's at home longer. A simple formula shows a possible cost savings of $2 million for the state. Here's how it works: 800 respite families X $157 average NH (nursing home) Medicaid cost per day X 30 days delay in NH placement X 60% of NH residents on Medicaid = $2 million savings in Medicaid NH costs.

I'm going to D.C. at the end of March to visit Senator McCaskill, Senator Blunt, and Congresswoman Hartzler. Although, I take the fight to Capitol Hill, each of us has the power to make a difference without leaving the comfort of home. Call, write, or email your legislators, especially when legislation is pending or advocates are visiting.

Become a voice. Answer the calls to action. By keeping up-to-date on Alzheimer's legislation, you can learn how to be an effective advocate.

It may seem that the answer to a cure is blowing in the wind, but if we chase it hard enough, we will eventually find it.

March Madness

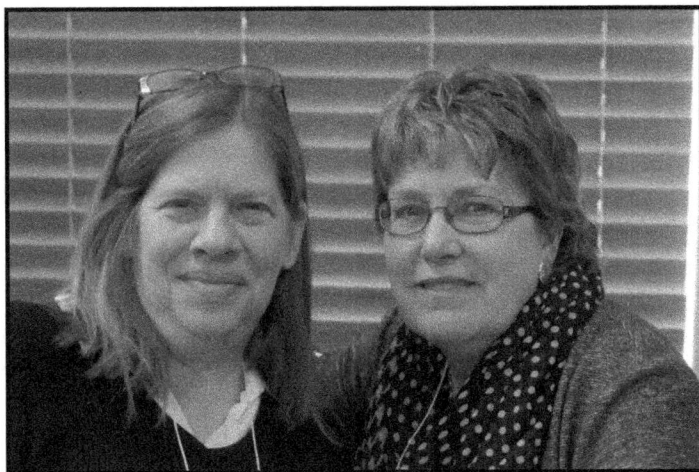

March marched onto my calendar with the purpose of seeing how sane I could remain in an insane world. The month began with a series of meetings. By Friday I was a little bedraggled and had driven to Jefferson City for the Business Women of Missouri legislative conference.

I arrived a little early and hiked from the parking garage to the capitol building to drop off an Alzheimer's packet. Oops, I should have known everyone would leave early on a Friday, so that didn't happen. I hiked back to my car and drove to the hotel by a circuitous route since I was coming in from another direction.

After I checked in and carried all my various bags to my room, I decided to relax with a cup of hot tea. I made the tea and opened one of those little packets with a napkin, creamer, sweetener, and stir stick to get some sugar for the tea. The cup fell and the hot tea splattered all over me, but most of the tea spilled onto the floor.

I looked at the little napkin. That was not going to work. I dialed "O" and asked if they had anything I could use to clean up the tea. "Just use a towel," he said, "and we'll send you up a clean one."

Relaxation? Who needs that? I spent my relaxing time cleaning up the mess. By the time I finished, it was time for my committee meeting.

Here it is the fifth of March and I've finally had a moment to sit down and fill out my wall calendar for the month.

Everything is on my phone, so my husband thinks this is an exercise in futility, but I like to be able to glance at the calendar and see what's ahead instead of waiting for a "ding" that tells me I need to be somewhere else at the same exact time I hear it.

With the two-day legislative conference behind me, I filled out the remainder of the month. All I have to say is it is madness indeed. I have exactly four days in the entire month that doesn't have one or more events or appointments. Madness! Or at least, what was I thinking?

I have several Alzheimer's events lined up. Monday is my Alzheimer's district meeting with Congresswoman Hartzler's staff. Tuesday is the Alzheimer's walk kick-off. I have two Alzheimer's conference calls this week: Ambassador and combined work group. Later in the month is a day for corporate sponsors, but the biggie is at the end of the month when I'll be going to the Alzheimer's Advocacy Forum in D.C.

To see all the activities on the calendar is a reminder that when I do have free time I need to be editing, organizing my electronic files, paying bills, catching up on my to-do list, fulfilling promises...and tackling all the other things that don't make the calendar or the to-do list.

A lot of the events on my mad, mad, mad calendar are fun, and the ones that are business are spent with people whose company I enjoy. Often, I spend as much time laughing as working.

With March comes the promise of springtime—flowers, birds, bees, plants, greener grass. Oh, yes, grass. Mowing? I'll think about that when the time comes.

Oh, come on. I know I'll have time to read a book, pet the dog, and maybe take a nap from time to time. I'm going to guard those four free-and-clear days as if they were made of solid gold, because, actually, they are!

March may be madness, but April will be here before I know it. I just peeked at April's calendar, and optimism aside, April is a popular conference month...

Lewy Body Dementia

"My mom has dementia," the woman said. "How is that different from Alzheimer's?"

"I think of dementia as an umbrella," I said. "Beneath the umbrella of dementia are several diseases. Alzheimer's is the most common kind of dementia."

In the *2017 Alzheimer's Disease Facts and Figures*, the Alzheimer's Association lists several diseases that cause dementia and associated characteristics. They are Alzheimer's, vascular dementia, dementia with Lewy bodies, mixed dementia (more than one cause—the most common is Alzheimer's and vascular dementia), frontotemporal dementia, Parkinson's disease, Creutzfeldt-Jakob disease (rare, can be genetic or caused by consuming products from cattle with mad cow disease), and normal pressure hydrocephalus.

The Alzheimer's Association does not list the rare disease Jim had. His diagnosis was early onset Alzheimer's disease, but his autopsy revealed the disease he actually had was corticobasal ganglionic degeneration, a disease I had never heard of. The autopsy report also mentions "incidental Lewy body," severe frontotemporal atrophy, tau positive glial inclusions in the white matter, but no evidence of Alzheimer's disease.

It is easy to understand with overlapping symptoms why diagnosis is so difficult. While searching for an answer to the "why" of Jim's dementia, we received several conflicting theories, including Parkinson's and Pick's disease, before physicians finally settled on Alzheimer's.

Of course, the mention of Lewy body in Jim's autopsy, incidental aside, had me researching Lewy Body Dementia (LBD). This disease affects around a million people in the United States. There is no single test to diagnose LBD, and in the early stages, it may be confused with Alzheimer's, Parkinson's, or a mental disorder. Diagnosis is made through examination, laboratory tests, brain imaging, and testing memory and cognition.

Through my volunteer work with the Alzheimer's Association, I've met fellow advocates diagnosed with LBD. I remember one man telling me that his hallucinations were disruptive and disturbing. Unfortunately, people with hallucinations or other behavior problems may be treated with anti-psychotic drugs. Haloperidol (Haldol®), olanzapine (Zyprexa®), and resperidone (Risperdal®) should be avoided because of dangerous side effects, including an increased risk of death.

Lewy bodies attack several different regions of the brain, which causes a variety of problems for the person with the disease. Short-term memory, perception difficulties, processing information, and language issues can be confused with Alzheimer's. Movement disorders are similar to Parkinson's with tremor and muscle stiffness. The distinction between LBD and Parkinson's dementia is based on the timing of dementia. In LBD, dementia will quickly follow parkinsonism within a year, but people can have Parkinson's and not develop dementia for many years.

People with LBD often have sleep disorders. The vivid dreams associated with REM disorder may cause a variety of symptoms ranging from talking while sleeping to punching a bed partner. A person with LBD may be tired all the time due to insomnia or restless leg syndrome. They may sleep excessively during the daytime.

LBD is managed in much the same way as Alzheimer's disease. In addition to physical, speech, and occupational therapy, the Alzheimer's drug Exelon® may be used. Other drugs may be used to help with movement, sleep disorders, and behavioral problems. The surgical procedure used to relieve the movement symptoms of Parkinson's is not used when a person has LBD because it may adversely affect cognition.

LBD causes a variety of behavior and mood changes running the gamut from depression and apathy to agitation, delusions, and paranoia. Managing the health care of a loved one with LBD can be quite challenging for a care partner. If you are caring for a person with LBD, it is important to enlist help from family and friends.

Taking care of yourself and taking breaks will make you a better caregiver. Do not neglect your own health! When dealing with a progressive, degenerative disease, it is crucial that you find moments of joy. Continue to enjoy activities with your loved one as much as you can for as long as you can. Convert challenges into opportunities to use your creativity to live life to the fullest.

For an informative publication about Lewy Body Dementia:
https://www.nia.nih.gov/alzheimers/publication/lewy-body-dementia/introduction

A Fleeting Shadow

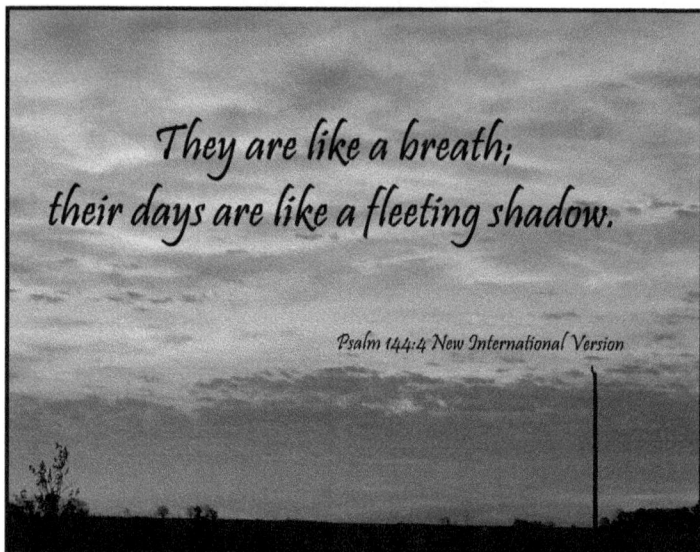

> *They are like a breath;*
> *their days are like a fleeting shadow.*
>
> *Psalm 144:4 New International Version*

At a funeral recently, the pastor referenced a book of Psalms that referred to life as a "breath" and our days as a "fleeting shadow." Sunday morning, I had planned to use these thoughts as inspiration for a blog post.

Before I had a chance to begin writing my blog, I received the shocking news that my forty-six-year-old nephew had committed suicide. I pushed all thoughts of writing aside and went to be with my mom who was devastated by the news. My heart ached for his parents who were going through the loss of a child for the second time. They had lost their daughter to cancer a scant five years earlier.

We had a discussion, my brother and I, about the long, slow process of dying versus sudden death. With one, you have time to say your goodbyes and with the other, you just hope and pray that you parted on good terms. One slowly breaks your heart, and the other is a shock to your heart.

Between PTSD and clinical depression, Jim was plagued with suicidal thoughts. It was a constant worry for me, and it was many years before I realized it wasn't my fault. It was hard to admit there wasn't really anything I could do to change it. I encouraged him to see a psychologist and to take the medicines that helped him function.

My sister made an observation. She said if someone dies from a heart attack, you don't blame them. If someone has something wrong inside their brain— thoughts they can't shut off, psychological problems, chemical imbalances—then maybe their death is no more a choice than having a heart attack.

We don't often choose how we die; it chooses us. When Jim died after ten years of dementia, I learned what the "long goodbye" meant. Although, death was a given, it didn't mean it was well taken. It didn't matter that I should have been ready when Jim died—I wasn't ready to let him go. The emotion that surprised me most was anger. When the breath was gone and his days passed like a fleeting shadow, I was furious that he had to spend the last ten years of his life fading away.

We all talk about closure, but I have to agree with my brother that closure doesn't exist. That isn't quite the word because some deaths just leave a big empty spot that can't be refilled. We just keep moving and hope the pain of loss will fade to a manageable level.

Lately, when I walk out the door, I kiss my husband goodbye—every time. "All the time you hear about people being in a car wreck without saying goodbye," I told him. I call it my "insurance."

More than insurance, it's a reminder that life can be snatched away in a heartbeat. We need to make those calls, write those notes, visit our loved ones, forgive, go on vacation, have fun, and make the most of each day.

We should be thankful for the time we have to love, dream, and live. Life is precious. Each sunrise we have another chance, another day, to right a wrong, lend a helping hand, or to make a difference in some small way. A breath. A fleeting shadow. That's all any of us have.

Headed to D.C.

In 2017, I made my seventeenth trip to D.C. to join my voice with fellow advocates at the Alzheimer's Advocacy Forum.

Essential preparations for the annual journey began on Wednesday with laundry. It seemed that most of the clothing I planned to wear was in need of laundering. Thursday, the packing began and I felt pretty good when I went to bed at midnight. My suitcase was full. Friday morning was going to be easy-peasy. All I had to do was make a few final preparations, grab my bags, and head to the airport to spend the night at a hotel.

The first problem was I shut off my alarm and overslept. I took the dog out and then it was time to sign in to get my boarding pass. My sign in wouldn't work. I decided to ask for a new password and my security questions weren't correct. What? I was giving the only answers. After much agonizing, I realized I was entering an incorrect password and once I corrected my error, I was in.

The few preparations turned into hours. I took my PC downstairs to hook into my color printer and it wouldn't work. I couldn't figure it out, so Harold came down and after a few manipulations, declared that I didn't have it plugged in correctly.

I hate it when that happens.

Back upstairs, I prepared to leave—about four hours after my target time.

"Just sit down and relax a minute before you leave," Harold said. "Otherwise, you'll forget something important."

"I'll go over my checklist," I said.

The checklist looked good. Then Harold started asking about this and that...he thinks of everything. Of course, he's the planner; I'm the seat-of-the-pants person. Eventually, he managed to think of something I'd forgotten.

"What would you do without me?" he asked.

"Go off half cocked all the time," I admitted.

By the time I headed out the door, it was raining, and the car clock told me that my timing was perfect to hit Kansas City right at rush hour on a Friday night. Oh, brother.

By the time I reached I-70, rain was pouring and the traffic was pretty well bumper-to-bumper. At one time, I looked in my rearview mirror to see a semi tailgating me. My windshield began to fog, and my wipers were working their butts off to keep the rain from interfering with my vision.

I called Harold for a weather report. "You should be running out of the rain by the time you reach Kansas City," he said.

The radio was on a country music station and I found the music to be soothing. I turned up the radio and karaoked to my heart's content. Once again, meteorologist Harold was correct. When I reached the city, the rain cleared just in time for a weird traffic jam on I-435.

Finally, I reached the hotel and everything was better. I checked into a beautiful room and although Harold had told me of all the fabulous restaurants nearby, I ate at the hotel. I was famished and the turkey club with "house" made chips tasted wonderful.

After giving myself a mani-pedi, I decided to make a cup of tea. First problem, no cups. I called housekeeping and that problem was solved.

I was darned ready for a good night's sleep. After all, the next day was going to be a long one.

After sleeping soundly for a few hours, I woke up at 4:30 and couldn't go back to sleep. I decided to make a cup of coffee and relax for a while until time to catch my flight. I poured water into the coffeemaker, put Coffee-mate in the cup, and turned it on. The pot stopped gurgling, but when I checked, all I had was hot Coffee-mate water. I had neglected to put in the coffee. Second time, I did everything right except I forgot to turn on the pot. Finally, I sat down with a cup of coffee and decided I would get ready and head to the airport.

After such a rocky start, the rest of the trip would have to be smooth skies. By mid-afternoon, I'd be in D.C. and have a few days to see the sites and spend with my friends. So, I grabbed my purple suitcase and set off for another round of fighting to end Alzheimer's.

Taking AIM at Alzheimer's

What is it that brings me back to Washington, D.C., year after year? It's not the cherry blossoms. It's not the Smithsonian or the monuments. It's not the food, although after a meal with my besties—Jane, Kathy, and Sarah—at the historic Old Ebbitt Grill, I created a hashtag: #eatingourwayacrossDC.

The reason I come to D.C. every year is to join with like-minded advocates who are good and tired of the heartbreak of Alzheimer's. We think it's darned time to find a cure.

Each year we are joined by an influx of first-timers. The Alzheimer's Association and those of us with the multiple stars on our badges do everything we can to make sure they are prepared for the Hill. Once they have the information and the "collateral" they put on their comfortable walking shoes and head to the Hill where many voices will share the same message.

I believe 1,300 purple sashes make quite a statement on Capitol Hill. As I went from appointment to appointment on Hill Day, we were the most visible group around.

Advocates from across the U.S. visited the offices of their senators and representative. The twenty-three-member Missouri advocates first appointment of the day was a coffee at Senator Roy Blunt's office. We boarded the first bus leaving the hotel and arrived at the Hill in time for the 9:00 appointment. That is, it would have been time enough except for the long line of people trying to get through security. As we stood in a non-moving line, we were directed to a different door so that we arrived in the nick of time.

After our visit with Senator Blunt, we split up. Some had house appointments and had to travel to the house side of the Capitol. Others of us, the "A" group (we referred to ourselves as the A-Team) moved to the Hart building where we would meet with Emma Kenyon, Senator Claire McCaskill's legislative aide. After that visit, several of our group headed home, but I had an appointment with Congresswoman Vicky Hartzler in the afternoon.

Our "ask" this year was two-fold. First, we asked for a $414 million increase for Alzheimer's research.

This is the amount that scientists at the NIH submitted as a "Bypass Budget" proposal. Based on the Alzheimer's Accountability Act passed in 2015, this is the amount to keep us on track to prevent or develop an effective treatment by 2025.

The second ask was for co-sponsors for PCHETA (Palliative Care and Hospice Education and Training Act). PCHETA (SB 693, HB 1676) is so important that more than 40 groups are working toward its passage. Nursing home residents who receive palliative care at the end of life are fifteen times less likely to die in a hospital. Palliative care reduces emergency room visits and hospitalization. This Act would (a) increase the palliative care and hospice workforce by establishing training programs, (b) launch a national campaign to inform patients, families, and health care professionals about availability of services, (c) enhance palliative care research.

Add your voice to our voices. Email, write, call your senators and representative to support research funding and PCHETA.

For $20, you can join the Alzheimer's Association's sister organization AIM (Alzheimer's Impact Movement). AIM (1) advocates for legislation to advance research and enhance care and support for those affected by Alzheimer's, (2) supports the re-election of our Congressional champions, and (3) speaks on behalf of the Alzheimer's community when 501(c)(3) organizations like the Alzheimer's Association must remain silent. Join AIM at the link below using my referral code.

Just a few minutes of *your* time can make a lifetime of difference for three of your fellow Americans who developed Alzheimer's in the time it took you to read this article.

To join AIM:

https://www.alzimpact.org/join/join_aim/code/1328a9afa5/method/link

Learn as You Go

At line dancing class recently, we danced to the song, "Life Is a Dance." As I listened to the words, "learn as you go," I was reminded of my years as a caregiver. During the decade of Jim's journey, I truly learned as I went along.

I certainly wasn't a professional caregiver, nor did I ever believe I would ever be a caregiver for my husband. His Alzheimer's type of dementia was a progressive disease where the caregiving became incrementally more difficult.

Becoming a competent caregiver involved a lot of baby steps. I learned the basics, sought out more refined information, and eventually I became creative. One thing I learned early on was that a solution that worked one day, might not work the next day.

The physical part of caregiving—feeding, bathing, providing personal care—can be hard, but it was the grief and emotional despair that I found the most difficult. The biggest struggle wasn't how to coax Jim into a bathtub; it was the heartache of remembering a time when it was "you wash my back and I'll wash yours."

Often, the small losses are the hardest to accept. I expected to grieve big losses, but chided myself mentally for missing the companionable quiet moments. One of the things I missed the most was having coffee and conversation with Jim.

We caregivers learn as we go. One of the challenges for caregivers is how to handle the baffling behavior brought on by a dying brain.

A three-step approach can be used to address behavior problems:

1. **Identify and examine the behavior.** Is the behavior harmful to your loved one or others? If the answer is no, consider ignoring it. Your two most helpful tools are *redirect* and *distract*. To avoid behavior problems, think about what happened before the behavior and what happened immediately after. Could something have been done differently to avoid the problem? For example, if your loved one removed all his clothing, was he too warm? Was he wet? Was his clothing uncomfortable? Become a detective!
2. **Explore potential solutions.** Was your loved one's needs being met? Could surroundings be changed to make your loved one more comfortable? How could you have changed your reaction?
3. **Try different responses.** Try to respond in a calm, supportive way. Your tone of voice and body language are more important than your words. Avoid treating your loved one like a child. Be respectful. If what you are trying doesn't work, try something different.

When dealing with behavior, remain calm, patient, and flexible. You will have better luck if you respond to the emotion and not the behavior. Don't argue with a person who has dementia. That is an argument you won't win! Sometimes the cause of behavior is something as simple as a side effect of medication, or an illness. Jim became combative when a new physician gave him an antipsychotic drug. He reverted to his normal demeanor once the medication was stopped.

Caregivers learn as they go. Being a caregiver is one of life's biggest challenges, but your reward is the knowledge that you have done everything possible to improve your loved one's quality of life.

Memories of Lilacs and April

The lilacs are in bloom and every time I walk out onto the deck, I smell them. Lilacs and April are two reminders of Jim. He left this world on April 18, 2005.

The lilacs reminded me of a story Aunt Nita shared at Jim's services:

"I remember a time a few years ago when Jim and I were sitting in the swing. It was in early spring; we had been talking, but not a lot. Jim got up and said, 'Aunt Nita, do you smell that?' He walked over to a big lilac bush and picked a handful. He brought them back to me and said, 'Smell this, Aunt Nita. Don't they smell good?' Remembering Jim, I always do, for I know he is one of God's chosen few."

When we were planning Jim's services, I took a yellow pad up to Virginia's house and asked everyone to tell me stories about Jim. I wrote the stories down, and I was still typing them when Gary Richardson came to our house to go over the memorial service.

Gary pushed the paper back to me and said, "Tell me these stories." I told Gary the stories, and he said, "Those are wonderful stories, but if I read them, they are just stories. You lived those stories, and if you tell them, they will come alive."

Rob and Eric both agreed and said that I should tell the stories. My first thought was that I couldn't do it, but after more thought and encouragement, I decided I could do it. That is if everyone put on his or her "happy" face.

Some of my favorite memories of Jim involved travel and music. Here are a few of the stories I shared:

Jim's favorite place to vacation was Estes Park, Colorado, and the Rocky Mountain National Park. We went to Colorado fourteen consecutive years. Jim was happiest when waking up on a cold Colorado morning, making a pot of coffee on the camp stove and cooking breakfast. I loved the cold mountain mornings too, but not quite as much as Jim did. I would snuggle beneath the covers in our bed in the van. Jim would bring me a cup of coffee in bed and sing the sleepy head song to me...

Music was important to the entire Fisher family. Jim was talented and could play the guitar, fiddle, banjo, mandolin—anything with strings. He enjoyed playing music with his dad, uncles, brothers (Bob and Billy) and a good friend, John Cook.

Sometimes music could get the Fishers in trouble and could almost cause fights. One time when Jim was playing his guitar, and Uncle Jewel was playing the fiddle, Billy sneaked up behind Uncle Jewel and goosed him. Uncle Jewel jumped, hit Jim in the head with the fiddle bow, knocked Jim to his knees, and gashed his head open. Uncle Jewel got mad, Jim had a dazed look on his face, and for some reason, Billy, who caused the ruckus, was the only one who thought it was hilarious.

Jim liked to hear Mom and me sing "Mansion Over the Hilltop." The words describe wanting a mansion, a harp, and a crown." Jim wasn't the kind of person who would want a mansion, or a crown, but he would want that harp, because it has strings.

I can just hear Jim playing "Buckaroo" on the harp. I bet Heaven never heard anything else quite like it.

Splish Splash

It was pouring down rain, but my cousin Reta was in town from Texas. The plan was to go to my mom's house at Versailles, and then Mom, Reta, and I were going to drive to my brother Mitchell's house for a jam session. My brother Jimmy and my sister-in-law were going too.

Saturday morning I called my mom. "Are we still going?" I asked her. My phone had lit up time-after-time with AccuWeather's areal flood warnings.

"Yes, Jimmy says we're still on."

"Okay, I'm on my way, but if water is across the road, I'm turning around." I'd always been afraid to drive into water, especially on Sinkhole Road where I'd lived until a few years ago.

Radar showed a swath of rain covering most of the state, and the entire area included in my travel plans were a bright red. As I drove in a pouring down rain, I noticed impromptu lakes in fields and ditches that looked like mini-rivers, bank full. My wipers worked overtime to keep the splish-splashing rain off my windshield.

After a grueling drive, I pulled into the parking lot next to my mom's and turned off the engine. The wipers kept going. How odd. I turned the car on; shut it off. Wipers swished merrily along. How great was that? I couldn't imagine getting out of my car and leaving the wipers running. I called Harold. "Take the key out," he said. The wipers kept going. I couldn't get them to turn off. The rain came down harder.

Harold called the car dealership, and they said I'd have to bring it in for them to see what was going on. Great. That would involve driving an hour back home. "Well, I'm going in to visit Mom anyway." I put on my raincoat and opened the door. The wipers shut off.

I crossed the parking lot and splashed through the water pooled on the sidewalk in front of Mom's door. "Well, I'm not going anywhere else," I announced as I removed my coat, thankful I'd worn my waterproof boots. My jeans were drenched. Mom called my brothers, and they were fine with the cancellation.

"I think it was a sign when the wipers wouldn't shut off," I said. The constant rain and "severe" flash flood warnings were other signs.

Sometimes, we have to pay attention to clues. Sometimes gut feelings tell you not to do something, and it pays to heed the warning.

I can easily think of several times I had gut instincts about people. When Jim and I were first married, a "salesman" came to our door and wanted to know if my husband was home. "Yes, he is. Do you want me to get him?" I asked through the locked storm door. I turned away as if to get Jim, and then closed and locked the door. The man practically ran to his vehicle and sped away.

Researchers say that our subconscious minds notice something is slightly out of kilter; dopamine neurons alert us to this. Bottom line, there's a scientific explanation why we sense danger. Our brains are our early-warning systems.

Jim was an intuitive thinker and believer in gut feelings before he developed dementia. Many of the symptoms related to Alzheimer's disease may be due to a massive disturbance in dopamine regulation in the brain. One of the jobs of dopamine is to regulate the flow of information to different areas of the brain to aid cognition. Some researchers believe dopamine is responsible for many of the non-cognitive symptoms in neurodegenerative brain diseases, including anxiety, depression, apathy, and mood.

A "sign," intuition, gut feelings, whatever you want to call it—I took heed. After I'd been at Mom's for about an hour, a bad storm blew through. Thunder, lightning, and a strong wind made us all glad that we'd stayed put. Out of control windshield wipers helped keep my trip shorter and had me headed toward home earlier.

After our visit, I returned home in a rain that caused floods, which in turn, were responsible for cars being swept away. I breathed a sigh of relief when I pulled into my garage and shut off the engine. What about the windshield wipers? They stopped immediately, as they had every other time until today.

An Eye on the Goal: A Cure for Alzheimer's

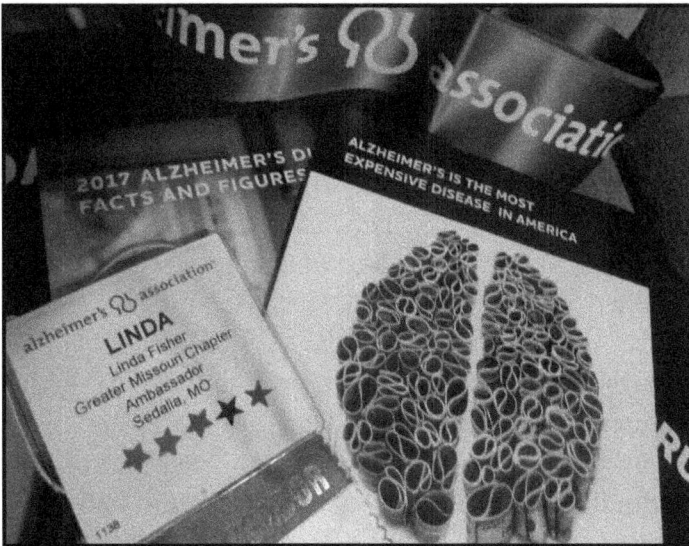

Setting a goal is the first step to success. If you don't know where you are headed, you don't really know when you get there.

The first time I went to D.C. in 2001, our local Alzheimer's Chapter Executive Director Penny Braun told me, "The goal for Alzheimer's research is one billion dollars."

It wasn't long before I discovered that research funding was way short of a billion dollars. Alzheimer's was pushed firmly to the back burner and funding was so tiny it barely made a blip on the NIH budget.

So year after year, I packed my bags and went to D.C. with that illusive billion-dollar goal in mind. I can remember being challenged with, "And just where would we get that money?" and "We can't 'earmark'

NIH funds." We inched a little higher, except for some of the tight budget years when we lost ground.

Things began to look up when the National Alzheimer's Project Act (NAPA) was approved in 2010. This act required the Secretary of the Department of Health and Human Services to annually update the National Alzheimer's Plan. The plan laid out a goal to prevent or find an effective treatment by 2025.

The Alzheimer's Accountability Act of 2015 required scientists at NIH to submit an annual Alzheimer's research budget to Congress. The scientists determined that if NIH would need to invest $2 billion in research to meet the NAPA goal.

It wasn't easy to jump research funding from the mid-millions to $2 billion. It wasn't an easy sell, and it seemed there was always a medical crisis that got the billions to stop them while the five million people with Alzheimer's waited for a cure.

Alzheimer's advocates are determined people! Alzheimer's disease costs our country $259 billion annually, but research dollars have traditionally been tight. In 2015 (FY 16), we received a historic $350 million increase. Once this increase was appropriated, the annual research budget was closing in on the billion-dollar mark at $991 million.

In 2016 (FY17), the Senate Appropriations Committee requested a $400 million increase which would bring our total to $1.4 billion. We celebrated with the appropriations chair Senator Roy Blunt at the 2016 Alzheimer's Forum.

Then, this year, we received the bad news that NIH's overall FY17 budget would be cut, and our historic increase was in jeopardy. We knew we were fighting an uphill battle to reach our goal. We weren't sure if we had been successful, but our champions vowed to fight for us.

Once the budget was approved, my inbox was filled with "hip-hip hoorays" as Alzheimer's advocates cheered the success of reaching our research goal.

In his letter to advocates, Alzheimer's Association CEO Harry Johns said, "This has been a historic week for the Alzheimer's Association, the Alzheimer's Impact Movement (AIM) and our cause. As you know, on Monday, congressional leaders from both parties and both houses of Congress announced that the 2017 federal government funding bill includes the largest increase in history for Alzheimer's research, $400 million. Today, the president signed that increase into law, bringing Alzheimer's research funding at the National Institutes of Health (NIH) to nearly $1.4 billion."

First goal reached (around at least since 2001): research funding of $1 billion. Next goal: finding a cure by 2025, or sooner! The sooner, the better. Keep an eye on the goal.

The Trip You Don't Want to Take

I was carrying my Mother's day potted dahlia up the deck steps when I tripped and fell. I smacked my elbow, knee, and scraped my foot.

It was a little shocking to find myself down, but I dusted myself off, moved my limbs without pain. It seemed the only visible damage was a toenail torn halfway off. I was luckier than my sister-in-law who had fallen over the weekend and fractured her hip.

Unfortunately, I had landed on the plant, crushing the plastic pot and breaking off a few of the flowers. We re-potted the plant, and I believe it, too, will recover.

These two falls made me think of all the times Jim fell. As I worked on his memoir *Indelible*, it became apparent to me that he had fallen more times than I remembered. None of Jim's falls resulted in broken bones, but he often had bruises, swelling, and cuts that had to be stitched.

Jim's main problem seemed to be balance. After several falls, he eventually used a merry-walker, a device that looks much like a baby walker for adults. He even managed to flip the merry-walker from time-to-time and the nursing home weighted it down. At one time, he was falling out of bed, so they placed it on the floor.

Up until the last several months of Jim's life, I was able to take him for walks. I held onto him, and he seemed to do pretty well. Once he began to tilt his head back most of the time, I had more problems keeping him balanced. Eventually, our "walks" involved pushing a wheelchair around the parking lot.

A myriad of problems associated with dementia can increase the risk of falling. Dementia causes problems with balance and gait, confusion, vision and perception, and, of course, the ever present medication.

According to the CDC (Centers for Disease Control and Prevention), nearly 32,000 people died from unintentional falls in 2014. Injuries from falls are the most common accidental death for older adults.

Six out of every ten falls happen at home. NIH (National Institutes of Health) has some suggestions to make our homes safer while we go about our daily activities. Slick floors and poorly lit stairways are two examples of hazards.

NIH lists these factors that can lead to falls: (1) loose rugs, (2) clutter on the floor or stairs, (3) carrying heavy or bulky things up and down stairs, (4) not having stair railings, and (5) not having grab bars in the bathroom.

If you want a to-do list:

- Remove safety hazards. It is easy to trip over electrical cords, clutter, dog dishes, or small furniture. One time as I was knocking down cobwebs, I tripped over a footstool.

- Improve lighting. Make sure bulbs are bright enough that you can see where you are going. Have a lamp at your bedside, night-lights throughout your home, and keep a flashlight handy.
- Install handrails and grab bars. Stairs and bathtubs are prime spots for accidents. Having something to hang onto reduces the risk.
- Move items to make them easier to reach. As a short person, I applaud this idea. Almost everything is out of my reach!

Having a recent fall makes me more aware of the danger. I had a really bad fall on ice one time and my first thought was that I was going to die, my second thought was that I had "broken" my head. Ice is another story for different season. For now, let's work on those indoor hazards that might catch us unaware.

The Benefit of Laughter

The 2017 Greater Missouri Alzheimer's Association's roast was a roaring success. I can't help but think a person must be quite comfortable in his skin to allow a group of people to "roast" him. Or as the emcee, Bob Pugh put it, "sear him" on first one side, then the other, before roasting him to well done.

I was assigned a seat at the "Hawk" table along with my new friend, Kathleen. We were glad to see each other since we were the first two at the table, and both of us wondered if we'd be seated by anyone.

"Are you a Hawk?" she asked me.

"No," I admitted.

We wondered what a "Hawk" was. "Well, if they don't show up, we can eat their desserts," she said. We were joined by a charming gentleman who said he was not a Hawk either, but eventually, the Hawks joined us—a husband and wife team. Everyone else at the table personally knew the roastee, Mark Fenner, CEO of MFA Oil, which made the experience even better for me.

Mark and the roasters looked quite dashing in their purple tuxedos. The evening was filled with good-natured ribbing, including Mark teasing a donor for selling a $10 million business, but donating "only" $25,000. The roast was topped off with a guitar and a sing-a-long.

Laughter as a benefit correlates to the benefits of laughter. I can't think of many people who need laughter more than caregivers. The health benefits of a good chuckle cannot be taken lightly. According to Mayo, laughter is the ideal stress buster.

A good laugh:

- Lightens your load mentally. Laughter relaxes you, and reduces your stress hormone levels, and releases neuropeptides to fight stress.
- Eases physical pain. Laughter triggers the release of endorphins, nature's feel good chemical.
- Improves cardiac health. The American Heart Association believes humor can help your heart by reducing artery inflammation and increasing HDL cholesterol. We have good and bad cholesterol. The easy way to remember which is which is "H"DL is the "happy" cholesterol and "L"DL is the "lousy" cholesterol.

Laughter is good for body and spirit. It gives you short-term and long-term benefits. Having a good laugh every twenty-four hours is just what the doctor ordered!

I easily stored up a week's worth of laughter at the roast. It was good to spend an evening with long-term friends I've met over the years, and with new friends I met for the first time at the roast.

I can't think of a better fundraiser than one that is fun. Beneath the laughter was the serious business of raising money to provide our chapter's outreach and to laugh our way to a world without Alzheimer's.

Decoration Day

In case I'd forgotten this was Memorial Day weekend, I was reminded by the bumper-to-bumper traffic in town yesterday. Our town sets between Kansas City and the Lake of the Ozarks so every summer weekend we are in the crosshairs of tourists. Memorial Day and Labor Day turn Limit and Broadway into parking lots.

I don't suppose most of those people are headed to cemeteries to decorate graves of loved ones. Decoration Day was established to honor Americans who died in wars, but has evolved into a weekend of fun in the sun and storewide "Memorial Day Sales!" Yep. The way to honor those who made the ultimate sacrifice is to celebrate and buy bargains. Memorial Day is most definitely a red-white-and-blue day right down to sales ads for clothing, hardware, lawn furniture, and every other consumerist purchase possible.

I remember when as a working person, Memorial Day was the first official holiday of the year. I admit that after our annual run to place flowers on the graves of loved ones, we spent the rest of the weekend pursuing some sort of fun activity.

Now, the highlight of Memorial Day is to attend the ceremony at the Veterans Cemetery in Higginsville and place flowers for Jim in front of the columbarium. Many of the graves at the cemetery hold the bodies or ashes of those who died fighting for this country. Others, like Jim, didn't die in the war, but as one veteran said at a Vietnam program, "I died in Vietnam; I just didn't know it."

That's what happened to Jim. Taking human life stole part of his soul and left it lying in the jungle beside the fallen. His life was never the same after he saw the lifeless bodies taken down by his M16. Jim had PTSD before we knew it even existed. When dementia faded his short-term memories, Vietnam clamored to the forefront of his mind.

Did you know that 3:00 p.m. local time is set aside on Memorial Day as a national moment of remembrance? At the appointed time on Monday, pause, remove your ball cap, and bow your head for the

1.1 million American soldiers who have died for this country.

Maybe a fun-filled weekend is the perfect way to honor those who made the ultimate sacrifice to keep this country free. It's a time to think about what is right about our country instead of what is wrong. This patriotic weekend is a time of remembrance. The most important thing we should remember is that our freedom wasn't free.

Go Purple in June

I was at the grocery store a few days ago and the woman at the checkout asked me if I liked purple. Now, how did she know that? Well, let's see—purple Alzheimer's shirt, purple bracelet, purple nails, purple shoes, purple purse...

"Yes, I do," I said. "Purple is the Alzheimer's color and I plan to wear purple every day in June for Alzheimer's and Brain Awareness Month."

Tuesday was a complete Go Purple day for me. Not only did I wear purple, I spent the day with Paige from the Greater Missouri Chapter on Alzheimer's related activities. First, we taped shows on two different radio stations, we contacted several businesses about teams and corporate sponsors, and we found a venue for an August program and care consultation. The day went really well, and I found the enthusiasm and support to be a refreshing change.

The Alzheimer's Association has a one-day event called the Longest Day. Of course, the longest day of the year is in June and this year, the fundraiser is celebrated on June 21. The Longest Day is about love for those affected by Alzheimer's disease. People participate in an activity they love—playing games, exercising, sports, hobbies—and while they enjoy their activity, they raise funds for the Alzheimer's Association.

The Longest Day is a perfect fit for the Alzheimer's Association. Caregivers can attest to the intensity and length of each caregiving day. The most well-known family guide about Alzheimer's and related dementia caregiving is called the *36-Hour Day* for a reason. Any Alzheimer's caregiver can tell you why.

By June, I'm always working on the Alzheimer's Walk and have never fully participated in a Longest Day team. I believe this would be a great opportunity for someone who isn't involved in the Walk to End Alzheimer's, but wants to help support the Alzheimer's programs.

Of course, I'd encourage everyone to participate in the Walk to End Alzheimer's. We are always pleasantly surprised to see people we weren't expecting show up on walk day.

Our walk committee has been small for several years. The same core group has faithfully taken on the task of making the walk a well-attended community event. As it gets closer to walk time, we hope to grow our committee. Many hands make light work. We've always been fortunate to have event day volunteers, but fresh ideas and new perspectives are always welcome. We want our walk to be better each year!

I hope you get a chance to participate in the Longest Day or a Walk to End Alzheimer's no matter where you live. You can go to act.alz.org to find information about the Longest Day and/or find a walk near you. You can help in many ways—you can volunteer for the committee, start a team, join a team, support a team, or show up on walk day, make a donation, and enjoy.

In the meantime, remember to Go Purple! When someone asks you if you like the color purple, it is your opening to create awareness for the five million in the United States who have Alzheimer's and the fifteen million family caregivers.

Silence, Please

My granddaughter was in a production of Dancing to Never Land, and I drove to Jefferson City to watch. As we were waiting for the program to begin, I remembered to silence my phone. While we patiently waited for her part, I took photos with my spanking new camera to make sure I could get quality photos.

An hour-and-a-half into the program, my phone began to play a happy tune. What? How could that be? Of course, it didn't play its tune during a set change or when the music was loud—oh, no, it was during a quiet time. Then, it dawned on me—it was my sunset alarm. Since we've been closing the blinds in the evenings, I don't have my bird's eye view of the setting sun, so I set an alarm to remind me to look. Turning off the ringer and media sound does not silence the alarm.

Last Sunday, I heard a phone ringing during the pastor's message. It rang, and rang, and rang. I don't know if the person was deaf, ignoring the ring, or not wanting to call attention to himself by pulling out the phone.

Maybe they thought it was someone else's phone. That happened to me once many years ago during an Alzheimer's Board Meeting with my first cell phone. I could hear a phone ringing and thought, *"How rude!"* Except, when I reached my car I saw I had missed several phone calls. My son wanted me to know that we were under a tornado warning. He didn't know I was in a different town at a meeting.

Then, there's always the talker that won't stop when a prayer begins. They are way too involved in a conversation to notice everyone has fallen into silence. How annoying that all you can hear is their conversation instead of the prayer.

When some people are alone, they have to fill their home with noise—the TV, radio, or some other racket—but I always loved the quiet. I've never found anything more soothing than the sound of silence, or the quiet sounds of a country night.

I'm not the only one who reveres silence. Others have provided poetic and practical observations about silence: silence is golden, listen to silence—it has much to say, speak only if it improves the silence, silence speaks louder than words, silence says it all...

I saw a TED talk on noise. Julian Treasure said that most noise in our lives is accidental and unpleasant. Noise affects us physiologically, psychologically, cognitively, and behaviorally.

Silence or soothing noises can improve productivity and improve mood.

After leaving a party where dozens of conversations are going at once, walking out of a noisy restaurant, or shutting off a too-loud TV, I retreat into my favorite environment of stillness and relaxation. My mind thinks, *"What a relief!"* I'm in my element when all I can hear are the blessed sounds of silence.

We Are Not Alone

When I walk my dog late at night, I always look at the sky. I've seen several mysterious lights. Some of them suddenly zoom across the sky, others disappear. What are those strange flying objects? Okay, a disclaimer—I do live close to Whiteman Air Force Base, and they do have some planes that look like they belong in a sci-fi movie.

According to an article I read in the newspaper recently, NASA is on a planet hunting mission. They have determined that ten new planets exist that have the potential to support life. They are in a galaxy far, far away, but the possibility exists that beings may be trying to contact us.

How many people believe our planet has been visited by "men in black" is somewhere between 25% and 45%, depending on the source. So, if you've seen something inexplicable, you are not alone.

Other than visitors from other worlds, we may sometimes feel alone. It seems we can live "down the road" from a close relative and seldom see them. We live in a world where many of us do not know our neighbors. We tend to go about our business and mind our own business.

When I was growing up, it would have seemed sci-fi to believe that someday the entire world would be a few keystrokes away. Who could have foreseen twenty-four hour TV, or so many channels that we never watch them all?

Still, in the world of connectivity, some of us feel alone. I believe many Alzheimer's caregivers feel the loneliest of all. In fact, caregivers may feel like their world has turned upside down, and they have landed in a strange and foreign land.

We each have our own road to travel; our own frontiers to conquer. We never know how strong we can be until we face an unconquerable challenge. For me, that challenge was Jim's dementia. For others it may be cancer, or heart disease, or the sudden death of a loved one. We never know what the next day or, for that matter, the next hour, will bring.

Earth is our home for a certain time. We have only a finite number of years to gaze at the stars, fall in love, have children, and visit with our loved ones who may live down the road or across country. We have things to do—so many things to do—and a short time to do them.

When I walk the dog and look at the heavens, sometimes I feel a chill, or an unexplainable ache. I see many things at night, and sometimes during the day.

One day earlier this week while the dog and I were meandering across the backyard, I looked up at a blue sky with a few scattered fluffy clouds. I saw a strange, rectangular white object passing rapidly by.

"Do you see that?" I yelled at Harold. Of course, he didn't hear me. Just as I marveled at that object, I saw another. In a few minutes, they were gone.

I told Harold what I'd seen, and he said, "Probably a weather balloon." Just like my dad, he thinks every strange flying object is a weather balloon.

"What I saw was flat. Didn't look like any kind of balloon."

Oh, well, there's no way of really knowing what the strange flying objects were. They could have been something from Whiteman AFB, a runaway pair of drones, sheets off a line that decided to go for a thrill ride, or maybe a deflated weather balloon.

Since the objects were unknown, I like to think they might have been a couple of angels making their way toward the heavens. Maybe, I was the only one looking up during that brief moment of visibility. At least there were two of them, so neither was traveling alone.

Company Comin'

My dog goes crazy every time the doorbell rings. She runs through the house trying to get to the front door ahead of us. We have to hang onto her squirmy, wiggly body to keep her from running out the door in her over-excited state. I think she's always hopeful that the grandkids are at the door, but she's ecstatic to see the UPS man too.

A few days ago, I took the dog for a walk. We went out the back door, but after walking in the oppressive heat, I decided that we would just use the front door since it was closer. Of course, the front door was locked, and I rang the doorbell so that Harold would let us in.

As soon as I pressed the doorbell, the dog began her happy dance and looked eagerly at the door. When Harold came to the door, she shot through the door running amok in her eagerness. I'm pretty sure, she was wondering who the "company" was, never once realizing it was us.

When I was a kid, I remember a song "Company Comin' up the Road." We lived twenty miles from nowhere deep in the Ozark hills, and company was a rare occurrence.

Later, when I became a part of the Fisher family, it was a completely different situation. It was not unusual to have several different families converge on my in-laws' house. Virginia was an amazing cook, and she could whip up a big meal on a moment's notice. She always welcomed family and insisted they sit down at her table to eat the mouth-watering meal she prepared "such as it is."

Family time wasn't limited to weekends and holidays. Any night of the week might involve a spirited card game, a jam session, or coffee and conversation. Company comin' was expected and an occasion to rejoice.

Times have changed, and so many of the family are gone now. Recently, Virginia's baby brother Larry passed away, so one less smiling face will be at the reunion this year.

We lived next door to my in-laws for several years. I always enjoyed the company, but being a person who has to have quiet time, I would sometimes slip away for an hour or so and go to my house. Most people didn't pay any attention to my comings and goings, but Larry would always smile and say, "You just had to get away for a while, didn't you?" It was as if he was the one person who understood.

Another time after Jim developed dementia, Larry watched the interactions between Jim and me. "It must be awful hard thinking for two," he said, having another insightful moment.

Life has gone full circle. Although, we don't live twenty miles from nowhere, we don't have a lot of company. Sometimes, the dog hears company comin' up the driveway, but usually she doesn't get too excited until the doorbell rings. Today, when she beat a well-worn path to the door, she was dancing with delight as she greeted the grandkids.

After playtime, she was exhausted and ready for a nap. After my busy, busy day, I was ready for a nap too.

Choose Your Battles

In Missouri, 2017 should be put on the calendar as the year of the Japanese beetles. Sure, we had some last year and they were a nuisance, but in 2017, they were a plague of biblical proportions.

These voracious bugs started on our grapevine—just like last year—then they moved on to the wild roses, blackberry bush, returned to destroy the apple tree and all the apples on it, attacked the yard trees making them look like autumn instead of summer.

It was a dilemma how to battle beetles. The traps attracted more, and it certainly was tedious to pick them off and throw them in soapy water. That might work if you had a scattering of beetles, but when they congregate in huge clusters and there are thousands of them, picking seems like an exercise in futility.

So we sprayed a little Seven on them, but mostly we hoped they would move along like they did last year. But oh, no! They were way cockier than last year. One morning while relaxing with my cup of coffee on the deck, I was horrified to see our rose of Sharon bush covered with the foliage eating monsters. "Okay, they have gone too far!" I told Harold.

I used the remainder of the spray he had mixed, and although it killed hundreds, it seemed that a legion was moving along the front line of the battle to kill the bush. Harold got serious and bombarded the tree with spray. That seemed to do the trick. We had chosen our battle and although they haven't left entirely, the remaining beetles lost interest in the bush.

As a person who is often out of sync with the opinions of those who surround me, I've found that choosing battles has become more important than ever. It isn't always easy for an outspoken, opinionated woman to do that, especially when so many have lost their sense of civility and respect for their fellow humans.

Choosing battles became an integral part of caregiving. When Jim was in long-term care, I could count on some residents' family members charging into the memory unit just spoiling for battle. Nothing was ever done to their satisfaction. Complain, complain, complain. I might mention that the biggest complainers were the ones who seldom visited their family member. Too often, it seemed that since they felt guilty, they wanted to belittle the aides and nurses that tended to their loved ones.

When these same people saw me feeding, bathing, or providing extra care for Jim, they would say, "You shouldn't be doing that! You are paying to have that done." In the first place (a) it really wasn't any of their concern what I wanted to do for my husband, and (b) I saw how overworked and unappreciated the aides were.

There were two kinds of aides: the ones that needed a job so desperately they were willing to try anything, and the majority who had a caring nature and whose job was less of a job and more a "calling." The people who stayed were not working solely for a paycheck.

Abuse and neglect of your loved one should not be tolerated. Show up for care planning and provide helpful input. Rather than ranting at the unfortunate person who happens to be nearby, rational conversation with the person in charge is much more effective.

In life, we need to choose our battles. Instead of waging war against fellow human beings, negotiation may be the key to settling problems.

On the other hand, an all-out battle against Japanese beetles is not only totally acceptable, it may be the only way to save your yard.

Use It or Lose It

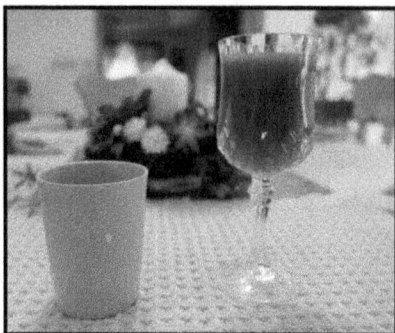

For the first two years of our marriage, Harold and I drank our morning juice out of mustard-colored Tupperware juice glasses. One day, I noticed some stunning crystal goblets shoved to the back of the cabinet. I knew they had never been used because they still had the stickers on them. Now, wouldn't my tomato juice and his apple juice look so much better in those glasses?

After using the glasses about six months, I managed to break the stem off one of them. I threw it away and took another one down. A few days later, I told Harold, "I broke one of the juice glasses."

He shook his head and said, "I bet I've had those glasses twenty years."

"Well, look at it this way," I, the optimist, said, "since we started using them for juice glasses, you've gotten more pleasure out of them than you did during the entire twenty years you had them." Really? How much good is something if you never use it?

Anyway, this little incident caused me to think about the expression, "use it, or lose it." That expression can be taken a couple of different ways. Like so many people my age, I've accumulated so much stuff that I don't use a lot of it. I basically flunked out of minimalist class because I couldn't seem to "lose" enough stuff.

There is another way that use it or lose it applies to our health. Lack of exercise is damaging to our minds and bodies. Oh, sure, we all know about going to the gym to exercise, but do we think about exercising our brains?

We lose a certain amount of physical and mental agility as we age. When we exercise our bodies, it helps keep us physically agile. When I was much younger, I went to a wellness seminar. One woman said, "I walk so that I am able to walk." She had severe arthritis and said that unless she kept moving, she wouldn't be able to.

When I don't feel like moving, I am most motivated to do it. A few days ago, Carolyn and I were walking into exercise line dancing class and we were talking about our aches and pains. But we were both there and ready to dance. Amazingly, I felt better by the end of class.

Mental agility works the same way. Use it or lose it. Keeping your mind active doesn't guarantee that you won't develop Alzheimer's, but it may reduce your risk.

We all know how to exercise our bodies, although we may not do it. You might be a little puzzled as to how to exercise your brain. As with physical exercise, if mental exercise isn't fun, you won't do it!

To decide on the brain exercise that will work for you, think about the things you always wanted to do, but never seemed to find the time or the motivation to follow through.

Here are a few ideas:

1. Take a class. Have you fallen behind on technology? Check out online or community college classes. Many colleges offer short courses on a variety of interests.
2. Learn a new skill or hobby. After going to a few "painting parties" my sister discovered she had an artist's eye. She's learning and expanding her skill canvas by canvas. I decided to try to learn to play the ukulele. I may never be great at it, but I have a lot of fun, and at least my dog enjoys hearing me play.
3. Read, read, read. Read for pleasure and for learning. With a library card, reading must be the least expensive pastime ever! I don't even need to spend gas money to read. I browse hundreds of library books online and check them out on my Kindle.
4. Working puzzles is another inexpensive hobby. I buy crossword puzzle books and Sudoku books at the dollar store. I also work the puzzles in the newspaper. Heck, I've already paid for the paper, so the puzzles are free. A good way for me to ease into the day is to work on a puzzle while drinking my first cup of coffee.

Exercising your brain is a way to lower your risk of Alzheimer's disease and enrich your life at the same time. Make your own list filled with things *you* enjoy.

My goal is to have as much mental agility throughout my lifetime as my ninety-year-old mother has. The only way to reach that goal is to think, plan, and take action to use my brain every day.

Beautiful Feet Carrying the Message

Sunday morning I took my usual seat for early church services. A woman came in and sat at the end of the same row. When the pastor gave us an opportunity to greet each other, I introduced myself to her, and she told me her name.

I recognized Laura's name as one I had seen on the Sedalia walk site. "Are you involved with the Walk to End Alzheimer's?" I asked.

"Yes, I am!" she said.

We had a brief discussion about walk committee meetings, and then it was time for services to resume. The sermon was based on Romans 10:15 (NLT) "...How beautiful are the feet of messengers who bring good news!"

I know that we may not see physical beauty when we look at our calloused feet, maybe marred with hammertoes, blisters, corns, or bunions. What we can imagine is the power of these "beautiful" feet to bring about change.

Each year we have about 400 pairs of beautiful feet spreading the not-so-good news about Alzheimer's disease. Many of the participants in the Sedalia walk have a loved one living with Alzheimer's. Others, like Jim's Team, walk to honor someone lost to the disease.

Many members of Jim's Team walk to honor other loved ones who have, or had, Alzheimer's.

All the beautiful feet are boots on the ground in the battle to turn Alzheimer's into a national priority. The walkers' beautiful feet raise awareness and funds to help families coping with Alzheimer's find resources to help them throughout the difficult journey.

At the same time, the Walk to End Alzheimer's helps the Alzheimer's Association fund research grants that explore new avenues toward finding a cure. New approaches, coupled with prior research, will hopefully build the momentum to find what has thus far been an elusive cure.

Alzheimer's volunteers are a special breed of focused individuals. It's kind of scary to me to realize how different my life would be if I had not taken that first step to become involved with the Walk to End Alzheimer's. Because of my volunteer work, I've gained dozens of amazing friends.

Perhaps it was merely a coincidence that Laura sat close to me Sunday morning. Or maybe, it was divine intervention to bring together two warriors to fight the Alzheimer's enemy.

As we left church on that beautiful day, we paused to talk.

"There's a woman on another team in my line dancing class. You should meet her too," I said. I hadn't realized who she was until our instructor Ruth had encouraged the class to participate in the Walk to End Alzheimer's. She told me she was already walking. In fact, I had just announced her team, Poppy's Posse, on the radio as the current top fund-raising team.

"I'd like to go to line dancing," she said.

"You should join us. We have a lot of fun! Our instructor Ruth is a joy to be around."

While we talked, people from the early services were leaving, and others were streaming in for the next services.

I told Laura the days and time of our three line dancing classes, and while we were talking, Ruth joined us.

"I heard some women were talking about line dancing." Ruth explained that the young man greeting people at the door had gone to the bookstore where she was volunteering to let her know some women were talking about line dancing. Ruth invited Laura to join us for line dancing exercise class.

Sunday was a day of connections with a dear friend and a new friend, both with beautiful feet to spread the good news that we are on the MOVE to End Alzheimer's.

Rest in Peace, Rhinestone Cowboy

At the National Alzheimer's Dinner in 2013, my mom and I were seated at a table near the stage. Our table was on the outside edge near some curtains.

"Rhinestone Cowboy" cued up and everyone began to clap in time to the music.

Suddenly, from behind the curtain, several people emerged. All eyes were on Glen Campbell as he brushed past us smiling and waving his way toward the stage.

Filmmakers James Keach and Trevor Alber were working on the documentary *I'll Be Me,* the story of Glen's Alzheimer's journey. They were on hand to present the Sargent and Eunice Shriver Profiles in Dignity Award to Glen Campbell. Glen was a truly deserving recipient. His "Good-Bye Tour" and the documentary were unselfish ways of bringing a new level of awareness to a vast audience.

Glen seemed humbled by the award. His voice broke with emotion when he said, "Everyone's been so good to me throughout my years as a musician. Thank you for helping me and my family."

We sang "Happy Birthday" to the country music star and helped him celebrate his seventy-seventh birthday. I brushed away tears as my heart broke for the years he would be facing.

After the program, Glen posed to have his photo taken with many of the ladies, including my mom. He was charming and sweet, but I could see his hesitation and hear his halting words as he struggled to adapt to his new reality.

His daughter, Ashley, testified in front of a congressional hearing on Alzheimer's. Advocates, wearing purple Alzheimer's sashes, packed the room. Ashley's emotional testimony explained the changes in her relationship with her dad. She said it was hard for him to recall her name. Their times fishing together no longer lived in his memories.

Two years after the forum, I saw the documentary, *I'll Be Me*. My impressions as written in a 2015 blog post:

It brought back memories of Jim's loss of communication and musical skills. At least only family witnessed Jim's problems and not a paying audience.

The Campbell family told of their struggles to make sure they walked the fine line between the cathartic benefits of Glen performing and being vigilant of him embarrassing himself. Audiences were tolerant. If he played the same song twice, so what? At least they got to see him perform.

Campbell's physician felt that performing on his "Goodbye Tour," doing what Glen loved, helped him maintain the ability to function longer. Sometimes his daughter, Ashley, had to tell her dad the correct key for certain songs. During their "dueling" instruments, her with a banjo, him with his guitar, she admitted that sometimes he didn't always follow along. Glen relied heavily on Teleprompters to remind him of the words to songs he had sung for years.

When watching old family films, Glen asked, "Who's that?" His wife, Kim, gently supplied the pertinent information: "It's you, honey," or "That's your first wife," or "It's your oldest daughter."

The film shows the relentless progression of Alzheimer's disease. By the time of his final performance on stage, Glen did not know it was his last performance. Cal Campbell said that when his dad performed, "He actually becomes himself again."

The story ended with the recording session of "I'm Not Going to Miss You." At this point, Glen is already fading away but his eyes sparkle when he finally gets into the song. This song really tugs at the heartstrings. The idea stemmed from Campbell's remark that he couldn't figure out why everyone was so worried about him having Alzheimer's. He said, "It's not like I'm going to miss anyone, anyway."

Glen Campbell's Alzheimer's story was heartrending and, oh, so familiar to millions who have lived a similar story. Today, August 8, 2017, Glen Campbell ended his courageous battle with Alzheimer's, and the Rhinestone Cowboy rode to his final horizon.

Total Eclipse of the Heart

I can remember a solar eclipse when I was a kid. We were warned not to look directly at the sun, but to use a pinhole in a box to see the shadow of the eclipse. Now, in less than a week, we are going to see a total solar eclipse—a once in a lifetime event.

So how this weird happening is going to shake out remains to be seen. I live in the area of totality. That means I can observe the eclipse in my own backyard. It also means that some of my relatives who live outside the area of totality are going to share in the experience by coming to my house. That is, if the roads aren't gridlocked with the thousands of folks from the four corners of the United States who plan to flock to the area of totality.

Watching the eclipse isn't something you do on the spur of the moment. If you plan to look at the eclipse, you must have proper eyewear. Before we ordered ours,

Harold researched the ISO ratings, reputation of the seller, and recommendations from the brightest minds in the world. His vigilance paid off since our glasses were not among those "recalled" due to being questionable.

All this talk about eclipses reminds me of Bonnie Tyler's "Total Eclipse of the Heart." I visualize a total eclipse of the heart as a heart that is beyond broken—a heart with a shadow hanging over it.

Some events in our lives can hurt our hearts seemingly beyond repair. When we lose a loved one to an accident, to incurable disease, or from suicide, life ceases to be the same. During the total eclipse of the heart, it seems that life will always hurt.

I can't think of anything sadder than losing a child or a grandchild. As hard as it was for me to lose Jim to dementia, I can't even imagine how heartbreaking it was for my mother-in-law. Our sons were grown when Jim developed dementia, but younger onset dementia or familial Alzheimer's disease can often leave school aged children without a parent.

In the United States, 15.9 million unpaid caregivers provide care for a loved one with Alzheimer's. Caregiving for a loved one with dementia is more labor intensive than for seniors without dementia. About a quarter of the caregivers responding to a survey reported they provided forty-one or more hours of care a week. Caring for a loved one with dementia is often a long-term commitment. According to the NIH and aging trends study, 47.4% provided care for more than six years.

Investing the time and energy to provide quality care for a loved one with dementia is the ultimate act of love. Caregiving becomes a way of life and when that ends, emptiness fills the space.

The concept that love can be a total eclipse of the heart takes on additional meaning when you learn more about a total eclipse. The world, as we know it, is transformed into a strange place when darkness falls in the middle of the day and the temperature drops dramatically.

Time becomes your friend as you rebuild your life. Much like the total eclipse, the shadow gradually moves away and the world is bright and normal again. A new normal, but normal.

Memory Trick and Tricks of Memory

As an Alzheimer's blogger, I think a lot about memory and how it often tricks me. My husband finds that memory tricks, or association, helps him to remember some important fact.

One day last week, Harold asked me to remember a number. Generally, when he tells me to remember something, I write it down. That is the only memory trick I know. It so happened that when he asked me to remember the number, I was outside on the deck drinking coffee and didn't have anything to write with, or on, for that matter.

"Okay," I assured him, "I can remember that."

About thirty minutes later, he said, "What was that number I asked you to remember?"

"Two-eight-four?" I guessed.

"You are close, but wrong," he said. "It was two-eight-six."

"Well, if you remembered it, why did you ask me?"

"It's really easy to remember, if you remember the first number is two, and if you subtract two from eight, you get six."

"Uh, okay," I said. I really didn't think that would help much.

My most memorable experience with association as a memory trick was a speaker who spoke at an assembly at the College of the Ozarks. The man, whose name I do not remember, walked around campus and learned the names of a few dozen students.

At the assembly, he had them stand up and he pointed at them one at a time and gave their names. He explained that he had accomplished this feat of memory by associating the name with a mental reminder.

Later, a student inspired by the speaker's phenomenal memory decided he could learn the trick. "Everyone calls me Capps," I said. From that day forward, he called me "Tops" because he pictured something on top of my head.

Memory problems can create amusement for those of us who are so distracted that we can't remember simple things anymore. Normal aging accounts for a certain amount of forgetfulness. My husband thinks my memory problems are because my mind is clogged up with too much trivia. "It doesn't work like that," I confidently assure him every time he says that.

Short-term memory loss is an early sign of Alzheimer's disease. Along with short-term memory loss, a person with dementia can't remember all the steps to complete a task. A strange environment can make this even worse.

One time, we were on vacation and Jim started to make a pot of coffee. The following excerpt from Jim's memoir *Indelible* explains how dementia can turn an everyday task into an ordeal:

One morning Jim prepared to make coffee in the in-room coffeemaker. He picked up the pot, set it down, picked it up, and set it down. He looked around in confusion trying to decide what to do next. From the bed, I said, "Put coffee in the basket."

"Oh! That's right." He added the coffee and then acted as if he expected the coffee to make itself.

"Put water in the pot." He put water in the pot.

"Pour it in the top." He poured it in.

"Turn the pot on." He turned it on. As soon as the coffee brewed, he was back in full form. He poured the coffee into the thermos, cleaned the pot, and brought me a cup of coffee in bed.

Memory is a tricky thing. As far as that pesky number, Harold and I were on our way to an appointment and he asked, "Do you remember the number I asked you to remember yesterday."

"Two-eight-six," I replied without hesitation. "What I don't remember is why the number was important."

Harold thought about it for a few minutes. Finally, he broke the silence with, "I don't remember either."

Remembering Jim

Today would have been Jim's seventy-second birthday. In honor of his birthday, I wanted to share some of my memories of Jim before dementia.

Jim's uncle introduced me to Jim on a hot summer day in 1968. I don't know if it would qualify as love at first sight, but it was darned close to it. He was drafted in September and after training, he left for Vietnam in May of 1969.

Jim liked to say he won me in a craps game. He came up with the idea that he could take R&R in Hawaii, and I could fly there and we could get married. The only problem was, neither of us had any money. Jim decided to take what money he had and shoot craps to finance a honeymoon. Sure enough, based on the roll of the dice, he had enough money to fund the trip.

We were married at Fort DeRussy on December 20, 1969. It was a small wedding with the chaplain, Jim, and me. The witnesses signed our marriage certificate before the nuptials so they could go home. Jim, being Jim, refused to wear his uniform for the wedding. He bought some "civvies" for the ceremony.

During the early morning hours of Christmas Day, Jim went back to Vietnam, and I flew back to the states. We began our lives together when he returned home April 5, 1970. He still had a year's obligation to Uncle Sam so we moved to Manhattan, Kansas.

The couple who had the smallest wedding also had the smallest apartment: one small room with a bathroom. We had no air conditioning, and I mostly remember the sweltering heat and the two of us sleeping on a twin bed. In early fall, we moved to a bigger apartment in the same house.

Jim was a family man. He loved spending time with his family and my family. We traveled home about every other weekend. We always drove an old clunker because Jim was a genuine shade-tree mechanic and could keep any vehicle on four wheels running well past its prime.

The army didn't pay much so we learned early on to budget our money. We always had a savings account for emergencies. Our entertainment was inexpensive. Jim would play his guitar and sing, we went for long drives, and we spent a lot of time at Tuttle Creek because Jim loved to fish. If we really wanted to splurge, we went to the movies or ate at Dog and Suds.

Glen Campbell's song said "Manhattan, Kansas, Ain't No Place to Have a Baby," but we were excited to become parents. Eric was born at Fort Riley Hospital and cost us a whopping $7. When Rob was born two years later at Bothwell, we sold my car to pay the $700 bill.

Jim loved to travel, and we often made trips to Oregon to visit relatives and his childhood places. Later, we went to Colorado every summer to camp in the Rocky Mountain National Park. Jim was happiest when he "had something to look forward to"—code for a road trip. He would pack the van for days in anticipation of our annual vacations.

Jim was generous to a fault. He would literally give someone the shirt off his back. He gave away valuable musical instruments to other family members. He was stubborn and wouldn't do anything that was against his principals. He could be exasperating at times.

Vietnam haunted him. He was mentally and physically broken by his time in the jungle. He had a fractured neck that wasn't treated until years later. He had PTSD before anyone knew what it was. He suffered deep depression and had to be hospitalized twice.

Jim was intelligent, loved to read, play video games, had a wacky sense of humor, was musically talented, and a deep thinker. He believed in ghosts, the unexplainable, angels, God, and that death was simply closing one door and opening another.

He loved with all his being and was fiercely loyal to those he loved. He loved his boys, his grandchildren, his parents, siblings, aunts, uncles, nieces, nephews, cousins, friends, and I never, ever, doubted his love for me. He called me his bride, princess, honey, sweetheart, but never called me Linda.

Of all the things I miss about Jim, I think I miss our quiet times the most: drinking a cup of coffee and talking about the mysteries of life. I miss the adventures, the comfort, and all the things that made Jim the unique man who stole my heart and held it gently.

Together We Can...

Saturday was my twentieth Alzheimer's Walk.

In 1998, the year of my first walk, four troublesome years had passed from the time I had noticed Jim was having trouble remembering basic information. Jim had always had an amazing recall for numbers and dates, but had forgotten his social security number. I thought that strange, but I didn't push the panic button until he admitted he didn't know his birth date either.

After testing, it was determined that Jim had dementia of the Alzheimer's type. Jim, of course, insisted he didn't have "that," as he referred to it, but when we saw an article about an upcoming "Memory Walk" in Sedalia, he wanted to go. "I have memory problems," he said. I had already signed up for the walk and had raised some money, but since Jim didn't have "that" I thought he wouldn't want to go.

We arrived at the first walk to discover we were the only people from Sedalia. The other walkers were Helen and Chuck from Slater, Joetta and Penny from the Alzheimer's chapter office in Columbia, and Penny's dog, Victoria. Six people and a dog, and I knew all their names—including the dog.

Saturday, was a different story. More than three-hundred walkers and thirty-six teams crowded into the highway gardens. We had professional DJ's, a super sound system, corporate sponsor booths, volunteer shirts, a professional photographer, and pinwheel flowers. We even had an official playlist of songs. At the first walk, the closest thing we had to music was Helen's hunting horn. The highlight of the walk was going into the VFW where a veteran asked Helen to blow her horn. After she blew her horn, they took up a collection to add to the walk total. The grand total was $600, almost all of which I had collected from co-workers and friends.

To make my twentieth walk special, my team wore the shirts from my twenty walks: 1998 - 2017. We knew they weren't exactly vintage shirts, but my niece and I laughed about struggling not to call them vintage. Old, I guess was the correct terminology.

Yesterday, Facebook posted a "memory" from twelve years ago, September 10, 2005. My son, daughter-in-law and their two kids were at the Memory Walk wearing 2005 shirts. I smiled at how small the grandkids were, and then I realized that was how small they were when Jim died earlier that same year. It made me incredibly sad to realize that they lost their grandpa at such a young age, and Jim missed out on seeing his grandkids grow up. Family was everything to Jim. He loved being a dad and was over the moon about being a grandpa.

It's hard to believe that I've been doing what I've been doing for twenty years. I logged my shirts before I took them to the walk to make sure that all the years were covered. Some of the shirts did not have a year and I had to look at photos to determine which years went with which shirts. Then, I identified the shirt by what it said: Move; We're on the Move; WALK (in Alzheimer's Logo).

After the walk changed from the Memory Walk to the Walk to End Alzheimer's, the message on the shirt conveyed increasingly positive meanings. The 2017 shirt, Together We Can End Alzheimer's, told its own story. When we work together, we can change impossible to possible.

It is shocking to realize that my kids are older than I was when Jim developed those first troubling symptoms. Time passes so quickly. Lifetimes come and go. There have been times in my life when I felt I was walking alone, but more often, I've relied on and been supported by others. Together, we can accomplish anything. Together, we can accomplish everything. Together, we can end Alzheimer's.

For Those Who Wait

We didn't get any decent tomatoes all summer long. Harold left for town this morning and gave me a call. "We have three or four semi-ripe tomatoes."

"Okay, I'll go out and pick them," I said. I walked out to the potted tomato plants expecting to pick a few and bring them inside. Ripe tomatoes were everywhere. The saying, "Good things come to those who wait" popped into my head.

You wouldn't think that I'd even think of this expression since patience is not one of my virtues. Sure, I have a lot of good qualities: empathy, a good work ethic, general optimism, and so forth. Patience does not make that list. Nope, not even as an afterthought.

My lack of patience gets me into trouble sometimes. I get really frustrated when I'm trying to open a file on the internet. I absolutely hate waiting for that little circle to stop spinning. Or for an ad to pop up and obstruct my view. Life is too short to wait, and wait, and wait. Often, I'll just close it and figure that I didn't really need to know the latest "shock and awe" news story.

Patience. I know men don't usually have any patience, but everyone expects a woman to have it. I used to have a certain amount of patience, but I guess years of budgeting my time has zapped what was left of it.

My saving grace is stubbornness, or bull-headedness if you ask certain people. When I don't have the patience to complete a task, I'm stubborn enough to see it through.

I'm starting to lose patience with a cure for Alzheimer's. People die every day from Alzheimer's and related dementias. We can't find a cure soon enough to suit me. I can't wait for the first survivor.

We thought about that first survivor at the Walk to End Alzheimer's this year. During the opening ceremony, we hold high pinwheel flowers in various colors to represent the walker's connection to the disease.

I always choose a purple flower because I've lost someone to the disease. Yellow is the color for caregivers, blue for those who have the disease, and orange for those who are supporters. This year, a new flower was introduced. Two young children held up the white flower that represented our hope for the future. The white flower is for the first survivor. That person does not exist at this time.

After the ceremony, they gave me one of the white flowers. I hope before much more time passes, I can take the white pinwheel back to the walk and personally hand it to the first survivor in our town. I hope to see our walk filled with white pinwheel flowers.

No, I will not patiently wait for the first survivor. I'm going to be walking, advocating for more research funds, and doing all I possibly can to push, cajole, and become the squeaky wheel.

Patience is not one of my virtues. I might as well make the most of my shortcoming.

Catching Up

Here it is autumn already. The season is catching up with the dead looking leaves on the trees attacked by the Japanese beetles. Hopefully, we'll get some nice fall colors out of the remaining leaves.

The yard is starting to look like autumn. We are surrounded by cornfields that have turned golden brown as they quickly approach harvest time.

Yesterday was the first day it was cool enough to think of dragging out the autumn wardrobe. At least it was a day I didn't feel like I had to wear a sleeveless blouse to keep from melting. We even had a gentle autumn rain.

I wore a hoodie this morning when I walked the dog. With her long hair, she seemed to be enjoying the autumn crispness too.

I kept telling myself that I need to get in gear and drag out my fall decorations. Last year, it was nearly Halloween before that happened. Unfortunately, decorating often falls into the "I can do that tomorrow" category. It seems each day I have a list of things that have to be done that day and can't wait until the next. Or worse yet, the things that should have been done last week...or the week before that.

Catching up happens every year after the Walk to End Alzheimer's. I have a lot of catching up to do. I tend to let everything else slide in the last few weeks before the walk, and often in the two weeks following. That means the last week in September and the first week or so in October are times to put on a different hat and catch up on everything I put on hold during the walk.

Every year I look at my September calendar and think…it won't get busier than this. Then, I flip the page to October and have to take deep breaths before I admit that I'm not going to be caught up until at least November.

I have several days on my October calendar double-booked and two days triple-booked. I have some serious choices to make. Throw into that the unknown, unexpected things that happen and October just got really, really scary.

I can't help but wonder what I would do if I ever did actually catch up. I kind of think that's never going to happen. Makes me think of what my sister-in-law used to say, "The 'hurried' I go, the 'behinder' I get." That just about sums it up.

The Ten-Year Leap

I can remember a co-worker who always said getting old was better than the alternative. She did have a solid point. Unfortunately getting older does have its pitfalls. A good day can be defined as one when something isn't aching. It seems that the older we get the harder it is to jump out of bed in the morning. I tend to drag myself out of bed and head toward the coffee pot. After the first cup and a few stretches, I feel almost human again.

It scares me to think that I'm the age now when Alzheimer's isn't even considered early (or younger) onset. Nope. I'm solidly into the age where if it happens, it falls into the statistical data as the age of greater vulnerability.

Although Alzheimer's is a disease and not a normal part of aging, age is still the biggest risk factor. If that news wasn't bad enough, two-thirds of the Americans living with Alzheimer's are women.

A gene called APOE (apolipoprotein E) regulates lipid metabolism. Less than five percent of the population has APOE2. This gene lowers the risk of Alzheimer's. The most common variant is APOE3, which does not affect risk of the disease.

The culprit is the e4 version that increases the risk of Alzheimer's disease. Most of us don't know whether we carry the e4 version of APOE. Jim's neurologist asked to do genetic testing on Jim and I gave permission. He had one copy of APOE4 and one APOE3.

Gender further increases risk, especially for women. A study at Stanford University Medical Center in California used brain-imaging studies to determine that a woman with one copy of APOE4 has a much greater risk of developing Alzheimer's than a male with one copy.

A study at the University of California found that women with a genetic predisposition to develop Alzheimer's disease do so at an escalated rate between the ages of 65 and 75. It is believed that the reason the risk increases for women in this age bracket is because menopause and decreased estrogen begin at about 51.

If you inherit two copies of the APOE4 gene, your risk is even greater. This too, is not a complete determinant since some who have two copies do not have Alzheimer's and some who don't have the e4 version have Alzheimer's.

People whose parents have dementia often fear developing dementia in their older years. My dad died when he was my age, but my ninety-year-old mother is as sharp as ever. I believe part of Mom's success is that she is active and takes almost no medications. In fact, we're pretty sure she's in better health than my siblings and I are.

The good news is that APOE4 isn't a doomsday diagnosis. The bad news is that I have entered the ten-year period when women experience a leap in developing Alzheimer's disease. More good news is that I at least plan to stay active like my mom. My goal in life is to find that fountain of youth she found and drink my fill.

A Lucky Mistake

I left early for grandparent's day at my grandson's school so I could go by and visit my mom. Delays can happen when driving more than an hour, and I didn't want to be late for the 2:10 event.

I had called Mom as I pulled out of the driveway. "Would you like to go with me?" I asked.

She was having lunch with my younger sister. "We'll be home by the time you get to town," she said.

When I arrived, my mom and sister were at Mom's house. We had a nice visit and a photo op before Mom and I headed to the school. We arrived at the school at 2:00 p.m., and I sent my daughter-in-law a quick text to double-check the grade he was in. "I think he's in the fourth grade," I told Mom, "but one year I showed up for grandparent's day and went to the wrong room."

My daughter-in-law confirmed that he was in the fourth. "We're here!" I texted.

Mom and I walked up to the door and pushed the buzzer. "We're grandparents," I said. The door unlocked and we went inside. A woman behind a desk motioned for us to come inside the office.

"Grandparents day is tomorrow," she said, holding up a flyer as proof.

Just then my phone buzzed, "Oh, no," my daughter-in-law texted, "it's tomorrow."

I immediately thought of Alzheimer's sign #4 "Confusion with time or place." Just as quickly I remembered that, occasionally, messing up an appointment is a normal age-related change. Whew! Dodged that bullet.

"This is what happens when you retire," I said. "You lose track of the day of week or the date." Today was the tenth and grandparent's day at school was the eleventh. Close, but no horseshoe, as the old saying goes.

"You are exactly on time," the woman said as if I needed some reassurance that I wasn't completely in la-la land. "You're just a day early. You can come back tomorrow."

"I have an appointment tomorrow," I said. Yep, for 2:15 p.m., no less.

"We have practice tomorrow," my mom said. She and other family members play music at area nursing homes, and they do a final run through before the week begins.

"Could we at least see him?" I asked.

She buzzed his room and in a few minutes, he came down the hall. We had hugs and a photo op.

"Enjoy visiting with your other grandma tomorrow," I said.

I couldn't help but think going a day early was a lucky mistake. I was able to spend time with my mom and saw my grandson. Grandparent's day came a little bit early this year.

Individual Results May Vary

How often have you seen an advertisement—weight loss, growing hair on a baldhead, miracle cure—where the final statement is: Individual results may vary. That is the catchall phrase to get the advertiser off the hook when the product miserably fails to deliver.

It is not just advertisers who promote the cautionary tale about individual results. When you develop a disease, you may often hear the same comment from your doctor. Along the way, they've tried to steer you toward the healthy path, but they know that some people defy all the odds, which they refer to as statistics.

I participated in a video conference recently, and the speaker talked about lifestyle as a way to increase your chances of attaining overall health for your body and brain. Of course, the ideal situation would be a strictly healthy diet, an exercise plan, and mentally stimulating activities.

The downside is that as humans we can't always resist the donut, we're too time crunched or physically drained for exercise, and rather than read a book, it's much easier to zone out in front of our favorite TV program.

Although population in general would benefit, we all know individual results may vary. We all know the person who smoked, ate junk food, and never left the couch for anything more important than getting a beer out of the fridge. We may write off these individuals as having a death wish, but sometimes they just go on and on until they reach a ripe old age. On the flipside, we all know people who eat right and exercise but develop cancer or die from cardiac arrest. Individual results vary.

Yes, there are exceptions to known statistical risk factors, but as the researcher pointed out: Most of us fall within the middle and how we monitor our health can make a life changing difference. Lifestyle may be our best defense against Alzheimer's disease and other dementias.

Genetics and environment play a major part in our overall health. If we are born with genes that increase our chances of developing Alzheimer's, we can't change that. In some cases, we can improve our environment. Where we are born and raised can affect our health throughout life. If we live in an area with air pollution, contaminated drinking water, or unhealthy living conditions, it increases our chances of developing life-changing diseases.

The bottom line is that no pill or treatment is a cure all for any disease. Hopefully, we are on track to find an effective treatment for Alzheimer's, but even when that happens, how we take care of our bodies and minds can make a huge difference.

When individual results vary, we should strive to make sure our individual results vary toward a positive outcome.

Chilly Days and Spooky Nights

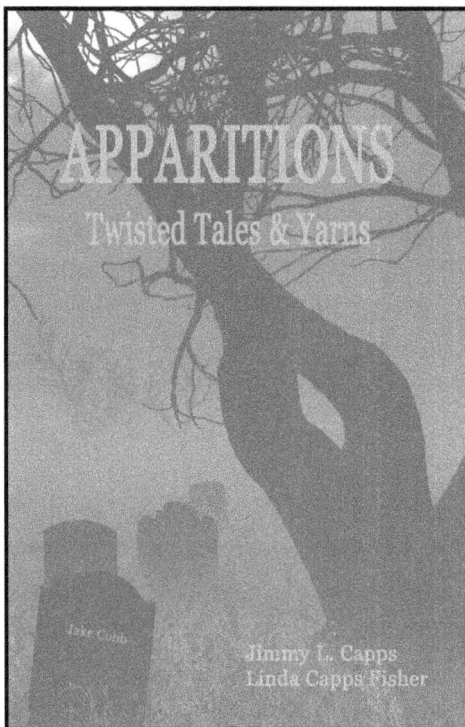

Fall is in the air, and when I take the dog out first thing in the mornings, I see frost on the ground and ice on the stock tank. Each day, I think I'm dressed warm enough for a winter's day, but haven't convinced myself that I'm to the point of needing gloves and a stocking cap. At least that's how I feel until the wind hits me.

Halloween will be here soon so my thoughts turn to things that scare me. I know I'm in the age group where Alzheimer's isn't even considered "early onset" anymore. I'm now included in the scary statistical risk for women over age 65. One in nine people over age 65 have Alzheimer's disease. The really scary part for me is that of the 5.2 million people with Alzheimer's, more than 3 million are women.

A few weeks ago, I wrote about showing up at grandparent's day a day early. Now, I'm so paranoid about appointments that I keep them in electronic form and write them on the wall calendar. Yet, I still second-guess myself. I've been bringing the music for line dancing class while our fearless leader is recuperating from knee surgery. I arrived early to set up the equipment, and no one was there. I glanced at my watch to double-check the time and saw that it was still ten minutes early. I mentally assured myself it was the right day. Eventually, everyone showed up and I breathed a sigh of relief that I was at the right place, at the right time, and on the correct day.

A few days ago, I opened the microwave and started to put the gallon milk jug in it. "Oh, my gosh!" I said. "What was I thinking?"

The next day, I shook creamer into my cup because it mixes in better when I pour the coffee. I opened the refrigerator, grabbed the milk, and started to pour milk on my creamer. Wouldn't that have been an interesting drink?

Yeah, Halloween is a time to think of scary things, like Alzheimer's and the ten warning signs of Alzheimer's: (1) Memory loss that disrupts daily life. (2) Challenges in planning or solving problems. (3) Difficulty completing familiar tasks at home, at work or at leisure. (4) Confusion with time or place. (5) Trouble understanding visual images and spatial relationships. (6) New problems with words when speaking or writing. (7) Misplacing things and losing the ability to retrace steps. (8) Decreased or poor judgment. (9) Withdrawal from work or social activities. (10) Changes in mood and personality, including apathy and depression. *

Scary behavior aside, this Halloween has been special. My brother and I finally put our twisted tales and yarns together into a book titled *Apparitions*. The goal was to have it finished in time for Halloween. Well, we made it in some respects since the e-book and paperback are available online. I don't have the copies I ordered yet. There was a delay while we tried to get the cover to suit us. Another delay was my reluctance to let the book go live because of my fear that I'd made a stupid mistake during the editing process or missed a simple error.

My husband assures me that my mind tends to jump ahead rather than staying in the present. It might have to do with mental overload. I have too many appointments, obligations, and an out of control to-do list. Multitasking has turned into multi-taxing on my poor stressed out brain.

Halloween is a time of trick or treat. I've decided to treat myself to peace of mind in regard to turning into an absent-minded retiree. At least with my optimistic attitude, I believe my occasional odd behavior is from being distracted rather than a sign of early stage dementia. At least, that's my story and I'm sticking to it.

Source for ten warning signs:
Alzheimer's Association: 2016 Alzheimer's Disease Facts and Figures, https://www.alz.org/documents_custom/2016-facts-and-figures.pdf

Veterans Day: Invisible Wounds

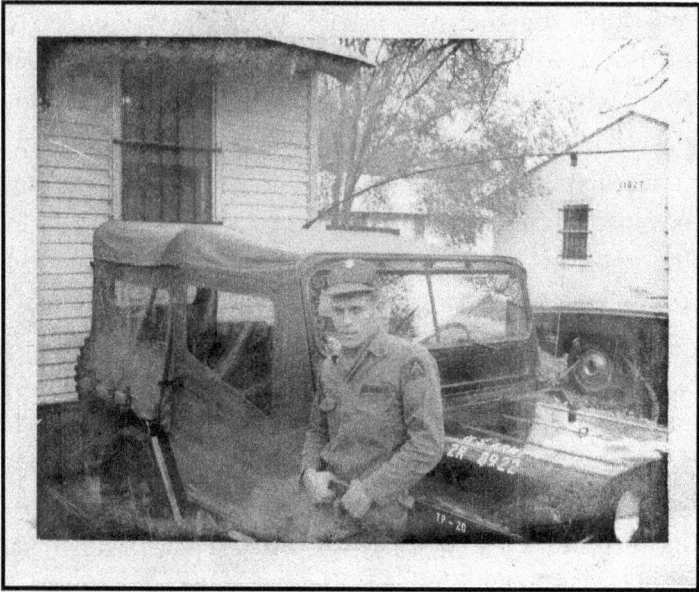

Veterans Day is November 11, but this year the holiday falls on November 10. At least this year, Americans will think about and honor our Veterans for two days instead of one.

The Capps family did double duty bringing the veteran's perspective to Morgan County schools. My brother Tommy, an Army Vietnam veteran, spoke at Versailles High School and my nephew Charles, a Navy Iraq veteran, spoke at Stover High School.

The reality of war veterans is that the majority of them are wounded warriors. Some wounds are undeniable because they are visible, like Tommy's wounds. Others have invisible wounds inflicted by chemicals and other environmental factors. Agent

Orange and chemical exposure during other wars can be passed onto descendents, abroad and here at home.

Equally debilitating are the heart and soul wounds that battle within. Twenty-two veterans take their lives each day. I hate to even think how many contemplate suicide or attempt suicide. I know that Jim contemplated it many times.

There is no hard and fast evidence that Jim's dementia had anything to do with his military service in Vietnam. I do know that he battled depression throughout most of his adult life. I also know that he was exposed to Agent Orange. I know that he suffered from PTSD, including flashbacks. I know that he had two complete mental breaks that required hospitalization. I know that he took medication that had long-term detrimental effects on his health.

Exactly how much Jim's military service contributed to his dementia may seem to be more intuitive than proven. Although I had no luck convincing the VA that there was a connection, science is beginning to catch up with my conviction.

Several studies on veterans who have PTSD (or PTSS as it is now known) indicate that they are twice as likely to develop dementia. When you consider that 30% of Vietnam veterans and 17% of Iraq and Afghanistan veterans have PTSS, the dementia connection needs to be seriously addressed.

Our veterans deserve more than a pat on the back or a "welcome home" in recognition of their sacrifices for our country. They deserve the best health care for all their visible and invisible wounds. As a nation, we have an obligation to reduce the risk of suicide, dementia, and other health problems with a connection to military service.

Veterans are the folks who laid their lives on the line for the rest of us. Some came home broken and it is high time that the government does everything in its power to make them whole.

Can we ever have war without fatalities and a host of wounded warriors? Will the world ever be at peace?

Until that utopia, we must take care of our veterans. Every day needs to be Veterans Day.

Source:

https://www.agingcare.com/articles/veterans-might-have-higher-risk-of-dementia-169916.htm

Heart Song

I was out walking my dog and the wind howled through the trees, making my face sting. The temperature hovered at freezing and the wind chill, well, was downright frosty. I cinched my hood on my coat to keep the wind out of my ears, put on my gloves, and shivered.

The wind made me think of a song I'd been attempting to play on my ukulele: "The Wayward Wind." In turn, the lyrics made me think of Jim. I don't know whether he was actually born to wander or whether he acquired "white line fever" throughout his childhood.

Until I met Jim, I never in my life knew anyone who had travelled as much as he did or lived in as many different places. Or in such strange places for that matter: "We lived under that tree" or "We lived under that bridge." I would have thought he was making it up, but other family members told the same stories.

Jim was happiest when he was on a road trip. I guess it would only naturally follow that when he developed dementia, he was a wanderer. It required constant vigilance to keep track of him. He would be out the door and down the road in a flash. He was restless and relentless in his pursuit of being where he wasn't.

When Jim's wandering made him too much of a challenge for his mom, my mom, and the hired caregivers, I had a short experience with adult day care. Jim took his guitar and amused himself by playing and singing—the same song over and over. I suppose the only ones who really appreciated it were the folks with short-term memory problems who didn't remember it was the same song he'd just finished.

Day care only lasted a couple of weeks. The day they had to track him down and found him on the highway, carrying his guitar, and headed toward home, they told me they couldn't keep him anymore. It didn't surprise me that even though he'd had enough of that place, he didn't leave his guitar behind. His love of music remained in his heart long after it slipped his mind.

The past seven days have been hard on the music industry. Della Reese and Mel Tillis died. Sadly, two music stars were taken by dementia: Malcolm Young, AC/DC, and David Cassidy, Partridge Family. Famous musicians leave a legacy of songs. No matter how long they are gone, their songs speak to the hearts of their fans.

A song can express heart emotions for us that we cannot express otherwise. Music provides a direct link to our strongest memories. My mother sings a song she refers to as "Jim's song." When Jim sang "The Way I Am," he sang it from his heart. One thing I can say for Jim is that he never pretended to be anything other than what he was.

Jim was happiest when he was playing music with his uncles or cousins. He often referred to these jam sessions as "picking and grinning." It didn't matter to him if he was playing his guitar, a mandolin, a banjo, or a fiddle. If an instrument had strings, he played it.

Jim loved the traditional gospel songs. I will never hear "Lord, Build Me a Cabin in Gloryland" or "Old Country Church" without thinking of Jim. We went to a country music show in Branson where several people played and sang old gospel songs in the lobby prior to the evening's extravaganza. Jim was already having trouble speaking by then, but he sang every word with them.

Sunday at church, the minister asked us to join him in singing "Jesus Loves Me." I fought back tears and sang along. When Jim was having a really bad day and I was trying to get him to sleep, I sometimes sang "Jesus Loves Me" to him because I knew he would remember that song. His lips moved and he mouthed the words soundlessly, and I think he found comfort. It was one of his heart songs, and because of it, he was able to travel in his mind to a simpler time and a place far, far away.

Free as a Bird

When I took the dog out this morning, a flock of birds swooped down to sit on the limbs of a bare tree. They were chirping and flitting around like it was a spring day instead of a prelude to winter.

What would it be like to be free as a bird? Most of us are trapped in some way. We are trapped by our mental and physical health, our inertia, our finances, our obligations, or other life circumstances.

I thought about Jim, who was ensnared by dementia. The hardest part of him being in a nursing home was knowing that he had lost his freedom through no fault of his own. Jim had always been a free-spirited being.

I paused in remembrance of my brother Donnie who died on this day in 2012. Strokes trapped him in his body, and he, too, had to spend his last days in a nursing home. Donnie cherished his freedom.

The biggest comfort now is knowing they are both free from the circumstances that trapped them in life. Jim and Donnie left their sorrows and afflictions behind, and they soar on eagle wings, flying higher and freer than any earthly bird.

Thankfulness

I woke up this Thanksgiving morning without plans. For many years, Thanksgiving meant going home to the Lake of the Ozarks. That's where my mom and dad lived. Thanksgiving was the one time of year that my brothers and sisters and our families gathered at the old home place. Since then, our family celebrates "Thanksgiving" in September at various locations, hence no big plans for today.

The memories of those long ago Thanksgivings crowd my mind on this special day. The table groaned with food, but if you wanted mashed potatoes, you had to get in line ahead of Andy and Derrick.

Jim always had his video camera. He "interviewed" everyone and one year shot a video of an impromptu football game. As he showed the video on the TV, his camera had captured the moment someone crashed into a small tree. My dad leaned forward in his recliner, pointed at the TV, and boomed in his "unhappy" voice, "Hey, that's the new tree I planted!"

Yes, Thanksgiving holds many happy memories, and a few sad ones. My dad was the one who insisted we all come home for Thanksgiving. "You can spend Christmas with your in-laws, but the only way we'll all get together is if you come home for Thanksgiving." The year my dad died, I had Jim stop at the cemetery to visit my dad's grave so that he could "see" me on Thanksgiving.

It was almost unbearably sad the first Thanksgiving after Jim was in a nursing home. That was a long, lonely drive with my mind crowded with memories of Thanksgiving past. The ten years living with Jim's dementia were the most challenging of my life. Still, laced throughout that time are many happy memories, loving moments, and tender moments that will always live in my heart.

On this Thanksgiving morning, I browsed my Facebook photos looking for one to share. As I went down through the photos, I realized that I am truly blessed. I looked at photo after photo of events, reunions, friends, family—old photos, new photos, old memories, recent events.

I have been blessed with love—unselfish and unconditional. I've been blessed with the best family ever. I've been incredibly lucky in love.

My life has taken some detours, but I know I'm in the place right now where I was meant to be. Of course, I have regrets, but overall everything has worked out and most decisions moved me along the path of my destiny.

I thank God that I've been blessed with an optimistic nature. It's brought me through the bad times and made me realize that life is cyclical—good times are always ahead.

No matter what I physically do this Thanksgiving, my heart is full of gratitude. I have health, love, and the best family possible. All is well.

Caregiving
Confidence, Doubt, and Little Things

When I was caring for Jim, I showed great confidence. I tracked his medications, I knew his health history, and we communicated on an almost subliminal level. Through classes, seminars, workshops, online training, talking to medical professionals, from the Alzheimer's website, and support group, I learned everything I possibly could about Alzheimer's disease.

Knowledge was my weapon against Alzheimer's. I tracked research and tried to get Jim into promising drug trials. The major roadblock we ran into was that most required participants to be at least sixty-five years old. When I finally found a trial that didn't have the age limit, they had a communication requirement. Jim lost his ability to communicate verbally early in the disease.

Still, I was confident that I could find the best medical attention possible, and when it became necessary, I tried to find a good home for him. Still, I was vigilant, on top of his medical and personal care. I offered my phone number as their hotline number, day or night.

From time to time, doubt overrode my confidence. On dark days, I would wonder if I was up to the challenge. I second-guessed some of my decisions. At times, I felt like a failure. From time to time resentment battled with fortitude. I mentally beat myself up.

Outwardly, I looked competent, but inwardly, I wasn't so sure that I could keep on keeping on. When things were going wrong, I would wake up with a cloud hanging over me. I never knew if it was going to rain, or if I'd be struck by lightning. It seemed that most of the time, the sun would come shining through. Often, nighttime doubts were simply replaced with daytime confidence.

When I took time to breathe, and think rationally, I realized that I was simply a typical caregiver. In support group, I learned that others had the same doubts I'd worked my way through.

I never intended to be the best caregiver in the world, only the best caregiver I was capable of being. In retrospect, I realize that I expected much more of myself than anyone else did.

When Jim first showed signs of dementia, we lived life as normally as we could for as long as we could. We cherished the good times. You know what I remember most from the nursing home years? I remember the walks in the park, the trips to Dairy Queen, the times Jim laughed, the kids and grandkids visiting him, wheeling him around the parking lot on quiet summer evenings, seeing his eyes light up from time to time.

Yes, I remember the little things. Happy moments ramble through my mind like old photographs capable of bringing smiles or tears, or more often—both.

Sights, Sounds, and Traditions
Of the Holidays

I'm not sure where the year went, but it definitely swooshed by. It's hard to believe it is Christmastime, even with two trees and a complete army of nutcrackers scattered throughout the house.

Holiday movies threaten to overflow my DVR. They all have a similar theme: a person who loathes the holidays, but magically "gets" what all the fuss is about. A Hallmark movie can turn the Grinch into a Santa's helper. Life is not a movie, and not everyone has a magical moment each holiday season.

Holiday sights and sounds greet us everywhere we go, beginning earlier and earlier each year. All that holiday joy and ho-ho-hoing can be a bit much for those who are dealing with the unpredictable nature of dementia.

Three important lessons I learned throughout my ten Christmas seasons as a caregiver: (1) simplify sights, (2) simplify sounds, (3) simplify traditions.

For most of his adult life, Jim was pretty much a Grinch about Christmas. He thought it had become so commercialized that it had lost its meaning.

In some ways, dementia made the holidays a little more tolerable for Jim. In other ways, it only added to his confusion. One year, I was putting framed family photos in a box to clear the shelves for Christmas decorations. Immediately after I cleared the shelves, Jim put the photos back where they had been. That was my first clue that he wasn't as crazy about the decorations as I was.

More than the decorations, I think it bothered him that I was changing his familiar environment. I learned to simplify the sights of Christmas. The holidays can be entirely too bright for a person who is confused. And it just isn't as much fun for the caregiver to do all the decorating alone and even less fun taking it all down.

Christmas can be a noisy holiday with traditional parties, dinners, and loud holiday music. When you combine dozens of conversations with music and piles of food, you are just asking for trouble. Communicating with a loved one with dementia is an acquired skill. Rapid-fire conversation is hard for a person with dementia to follow and can bring about a negative reaction. Replace noisy gatherings with soothing traditional music your loved one will remember from his or her childhood.

Simplify traditions by getting rid of the ones you have clung to through a sense of obligation. If you don't enjoy it, don't expect your loved one to tolerate it. Do the things that make you happy. If your idea of a good Christmas is a quiet evening at home, then do it. Most of the stress of Christmas is caused by trying to meet the expectations of other people. Those who truly care about you are not going to want to add any more stress to your life.

Simplifying your holiday can bring the joy back to the season. The spirit of Christmas isn't wrapped up in glittery packages or found in a department store. The spirit of Christmas is a child wrapped in swaddling clothing, placed in a manger. The spirit of Christmas is love, peace, and a light that shines within our hearts and souls.

Slaying Dragons

An old story came to my mind this morning: a man asked his friend with a terminal disease, "How does it feel to know you are dying?" The friend responded, "How do you feel to think you are not?"

How you cope with terminal disease depends on how you feel about battling dragons. You can meet the dragon head on, or you can turn tail and run. Fight or flight. It depends on the kind of person you are.

Alzheimer's is a big, ugly fire-breathing dragon of a disease. It is a terminal disease that can take a decade or more to reach its ultimate conclusion. That's entirely too long to be in "dying" mode.

As if having a terminal disease isn't enough of a problem, people often have more than one potentially fatal condition. Heart disease, diabetes, kidney disease, cancer…the list goes on and on. While you are battling the big dragon, smaller potentially dangerous dragons are coming at you from every side.

In real life, you battle diseases as if you were fighting those mythical dragons, that is, one at a time. Otherwise, it is overwhelming.

When Jim developed other medical problems, we dealt with them as they came. I decided it was best to address each issue as it arrived. My thoughts were to keep him as healthy and mobile as possible.

Alzheimer's is a disease that affects every person in the family. It may affect them in different ways. One person steps up to be the caregiver—usually a spouse or child. Some may withdraw while others go into overdrive to provide support for the primary caregiver.

Then, there's Mr. or Ms. Know-it-All who don't really want to do anything but tell everyone else how to do it. Yes, the personalities of those involved can be quite challenging.

Ultimately, the biggest choice is whether to give up or go slay the dragon. When you give up, you waste precious time. Chronic illness of any type becomes a dragon that needs to be slain.

If you look at what you still have instead of what you've lost, you can begin to enjoy life. Cherish those little moments of joy, and make memories. You don't want to lose a decade of your life seeing only the doom and gloom of a terminal disease. Become a dragon slayer!

Kathy Siggins Stamps out Alzheimer's

I went to my local post office this week and bought a sheet of Alzheimer's semipostal stamps. I couldn't help but brag, "My friend, Kathy Siggins, is the one who got the approval for this stamp. She worked eighteen years to make it happen!"

Often, we claim people as friends when they do something extraordinary—something that makes a mark in history. In this case, I wasn't exaggerating. I met Sarah Harris, Jane Adams, and Kathy Siggins at the first Alzheimer's forum I went to in 2001. We forged a lasting and special friendship of the heart.

And guess what? Kathy was already working on the Alzheimer's semipostal stamp, and was still working on it at the 2017 forum.

Well, frankly, I didn't even know what a semipostal stamp was, or why we wanted, much less needed, an Alzheimer's stamp. Since then, thanks to my friend Kathy, I've learned quite a bit about them.

Getting a semi-postal stamp approved isn't easy. As you've heard said before…it takes an Act of Congress. The Semipostal Authorization Act grants the U.S. Postal Service authority to sell fundraising stamps to further causes that are in the national interest. They will issue five semipostal stamps over the next ten years, with the Alzheimer's stamp being the first discretionary semipostal stamp. The second stamp, already approved, is another cause near-and-dear to me: Post Traumatic Stress Disorder semipostal stamp.

Why are these stamps important? Prior semipostal stamps have raised millions of dollars. Congress mandated the first semipostal stamp in history for Breast Cancer Research, which raised $86.7 million and a Save Vanishing Species semipostal stamp that raised $4.3 million.

The Alzheimer's stamp costs sixty cents. The additional cost of the stamp will go toward Alzheimer's research. As Congressman Elijah Cummings said at the dedication, this is a "big deal."

Kathy Siggins has been busy lately. The stamp was released on November 30 and she was a special guest at the official dedication of the stamp. The Congressman recognized Kathy for her work. "You turned your pain into a passion and to a purpose." He said it would affect generations yet unborn. He went on to say, "Your name may never appear on the front page of the Washington Post. You may not even make the local gazette... By the way, you may never be famous, but there will be people who will benefit from what you did."

The Congressman said Kathy was an example of how "one person who instead of standing on the sidelines of life having a pity party" used her energy to make life better for somebody else.

I've followed Kathy's various events online: award presentations, television interviews, dedication parties, and celebrations. She takes it all in stride. Kathy has worked toward this day for so long, I'm sure she is filled with exhilaration.

The stamp, thanks to the unwavering efforts of Kathy Siggins, will be on sale for two years. Buy early and often! Let this be the only stamp you buy in the next two years.

Yes, Kathy, you are our Alzheimer's hero. Speaking for Sarah, Jane, and myself, we salute you, our sister of the heart, and heap our gratitude and love on you for being the special person you are.

The US Postal Service dedication ceremony:
https://www.facebook.com/USPS/videos/10155960281864810/

Christmas at the Home

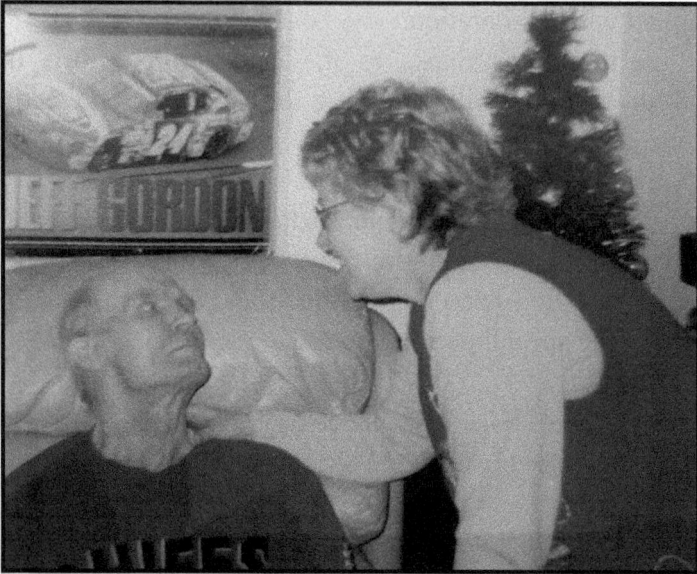

I saw a post this morning, "Please, if you have loved ones in a nursing home try to spend some time with them." This reminder made me think of the five Christmas holidays Jim spent in a nursing home.

One of the disturbing trends I noticed at the nursing home was the lack of family support, especially in the special care unit. Excuses ranged from "he doesn't know me" to "I can't stand to see her that way."

The family who never visited missed the smiles and bright eyes when a loved one walked through the door. When I visited Jim, some of the other residents felt that I was there to see them too. I greeted them by name, commented on how pretty someone's dress was, or offered to get the attention of an aide when they pleaded, "Will you help me?"

"They won't let me help you, but I can get someone who will," I told them.

Christmas time seemed a particularly lonesome time at the nursing home while families celebrated at home. I was looking through some of my Christmas memories in *Indelible* (memoir in progress). I decided to share some of those memories.

Home for Christmas:

Around Christmas time, we drove around town after dark to see the lights. The state school had an outstanding display with Christmas scenes set up in small buildings. Christmas music played on loudspeakers throughout the drive. Eric, Shawna, and the grandkids enjoyed riding through the light display too.

I brought Jim home for Whitney's birthday party and our annual Christmas Eve get-together. After our Christmas Eve celebration, we drove Jim through the Christmas lights before returning him to the nursing home.

On Christmas day, I picked him up to have dinner at his mom's house.

We made it through our first Christmas with Jim living in a nursing home by making it as close as possible to our normal celebration.

Home for another Christmas:

I brought Jim home and helped him out of the van and down the walkway. He took his usual seat on the reclining section of the couch.

Rob and Colby were playing video games on the TV. Before long, he yelled, "Hey!" and jumped up and started going toward them.

"I wonder if he wants to play," I said. At one time, Jim loved video games, and he played Mario Karts long after he developed dementia.

Rob ejected the game they were playing, and inserted Mario Karts into the Play Station.

"Here, Dad," he said as he handed Jim a control. Jim didn't seem to remember how to use it, so Rob passed the other control to Colby and helped his dad maneuver the one he held.

After a few races, Jim remembered how to run the car around the track, but the master of the game was not competitive.

Christmas at the Home:

I wanted to bring Jim home for Christmas Eve, but it was snowing, so I decided it wasn't a good idea. Christmas Day, I brought Jim a bowl of the chili Rob made for Christmas Eve. He ate the chili and the ham that came on his plate.

While Jim was in the nursing home, the staff and I did everything we could to make the holiday special. They decorated for Christmas and provided Christmas cards that they taped to the doors. I brought a tree and decorated his room.

The staff drew names and gave Christmas presents to the residents. Jim was wearing his gift, a Dale Earnhardt, Jr. shirt.

I had planned to take down his Christmas tree, but the box was still in the car where I had forgotten it. The rain pelted against Jim's windows, and I dreaded going back outside.

As I spooned his food, I talked to him. "Well, I'm not going back out in that crap to get the box for the Christmas tree." Jim's eyes moved toward the tree. "I guess you'll get to enjoy it one more day."

We spent fifteen minutes together Christmas Day 1969 before Jim returned to Vietnam and I flew home. From then until Jim passed away, we were together every Christmas Day. I cherish the memories of our Christmases regardless of the setting.

Cold Is for the Bold

As 2017 winds down, winter has barely started, and I'm ready for spring.

With the cold weather and sub-zero wind chills lately, I've had to psych myself up every time I head out the door to walk the dog. When my husband asked, "What do you want for Christmas?" the only thing I could think of was an N-Ferno hood like he bought for himself last year.

Now, I dress as if I'm going on a polar expedition every time I walk out the door. As with everything, it seems, there is an upside and downside to the new hood. The cold doesn't make my face hurt anymore, but my glasses fog up and I have to remove them. As nearsighted as I am, that means I can't see much. Still, the hood makes me feel like a Ninja warrior battling the cold.

The best defense against the cold is layering. I bought a pair of fleece-lined sweatpants, but they didn't stop the cold until I wore my Cuddle Duds beneath them.

This New Year's Eve, not only our bodies are layered against the cold, our souls and hearts are layered to shield us from hurt and disappointments. In order to overcome the challenges we face on a daily basis, we have to pile on layers of accomplishment. To defeat sadness, we need to find joy. To defend ourselves against the darkness, we need to seek out light.

As we reflect on the dying year, we can focus on the bad or sad times, or we can laser our thoughts on the good times. The same could be said for the past years. A lifetime of years.

For some reason this morning, I found myself dwelling on my failures and missteps. As I thought about the times I made stupid mistakes, I found myself sinking into a place I didn't want to be. Then, I went on with my day—breakfast, laundry, walking the dog— those little daily obligations that are there to be done again and again. There's nothing permanent to be gained or lost.

As I worked on Jim's memoir *Indelible*, I found myself laughing and crying as I relived that period of my life. The thing is that life is cyclical. Maybe, roller coaster would be a better description. High highs, low lows, sudden drops, heart-stopping curves, and the moment of quiet and relief when one ride ends and before the next one begins.

Tomorrow begins a new year. I've never been much of one for making resolutions because I never saw a resolution that I couldn't break within a few days. Instead, I'm looking at more of an overview.

Over the past several months, I've been paring down my outside obligations. This is a real effort on my part to free up more of my time to tend to matters important to me.

One thing for sure, 2018 is going to have a cold, cold start. So tomorrow, when I don my Ninja hood, I'll battle the cold and face the new year with boldness and optimism. After all, the hood keeps the wind from hurting my face, and spring will be only seventy-seven days away.

Alzheimer's Anthology of Unconditional Love

Edited by L. S. Fisher

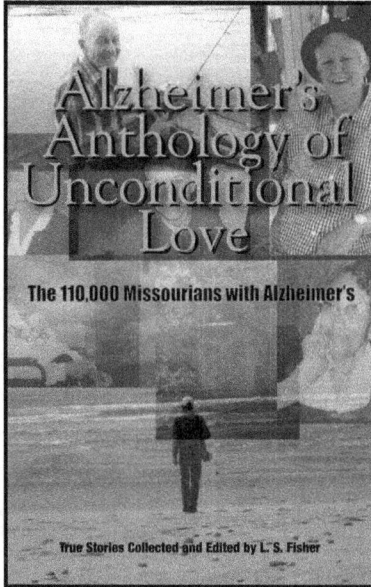

Mozark Press
PO Box 1746
Sedalia, MO 65302

www.MozarkPress.com
www.lsfisher.com

Early Onset Blog: Essays from an Online Journal

By L. S. Fisher

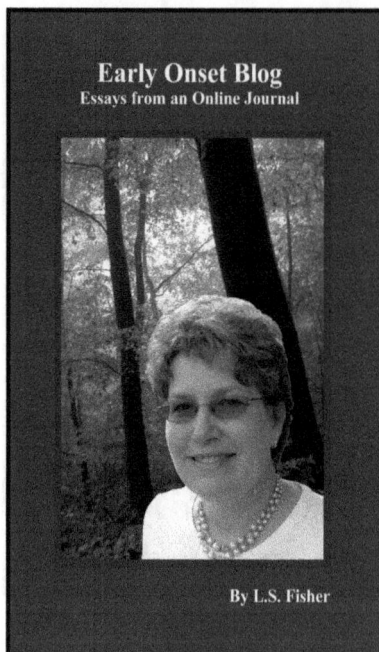

Mozark Press
PO Box 1746
Sedalia, MO 65302

www.MozarkPress.com
www.lsfisher.com

Early Onset Blog: The Friendship Connection
&
Other Essays

By L. S. Fisher

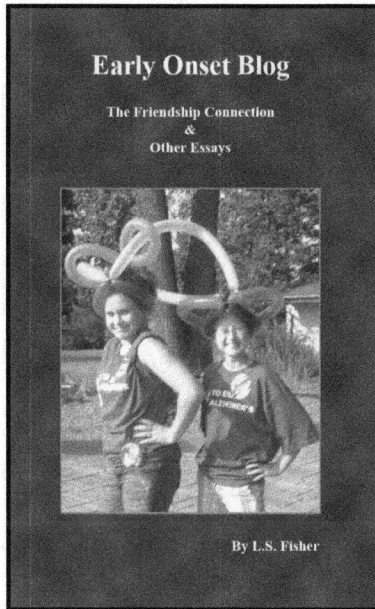

Early Onset Blog

The Friendship Connection
&
Other Essays

By L.S. Fisher

Mozark Press
PO Box 1746
Sedalia, MO 65302

www.MozarkPress.com
www.lsfisher.com

Early Onset Alzheimer's
Encourage, Inspire, and Inform

By L. S. Fisher

Mozark Press
PO Box 1746
Sedalia, MO 65302

www.MozarkPress.com
www.lsfisher.com

Early Onset Alzheimer's
My Recollections, Our Memories

By L. S. Fisher

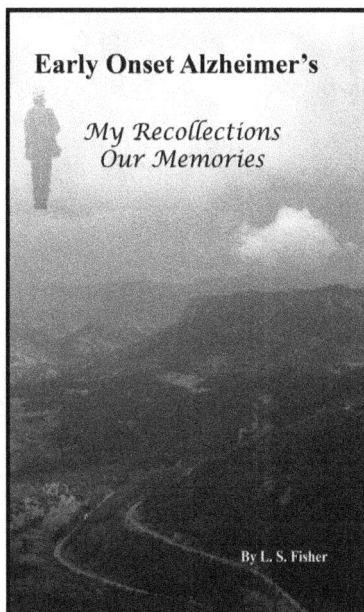

Mozark Press
PO Box 1746
Sedalia, MO 65302

www.MozarkPress.com
www.lsfisher.com

Focus on the Positive
Inspire, Encourage, and Inform

By L. S. Fisher

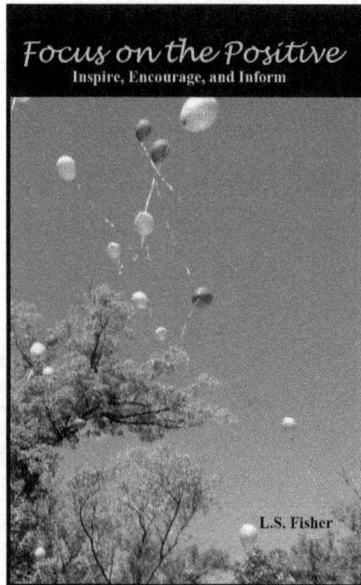

Mozark Press
PO Box 1746
Sedalia, MO 65302

www.MozarkPress.com
www.lsfisher.com

Garden of Hope
Growing Alzheimer's Awareness

By L. S. Fisher

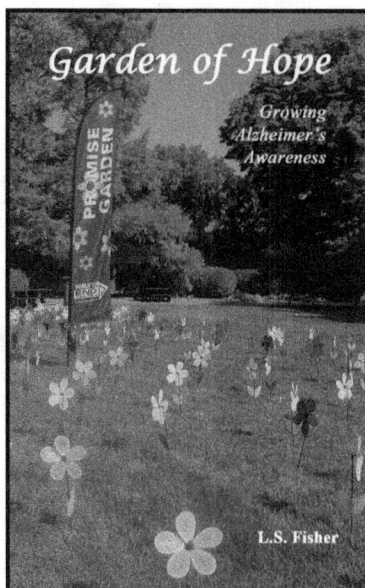

Mozark Press
PO Box 1746
Sedalia, MO 65302

www.MozarkPress.com
www.lsfisher.com

The Broken Road
Navigating the Alzheimer's Labyrinth

By L. S. Fisher

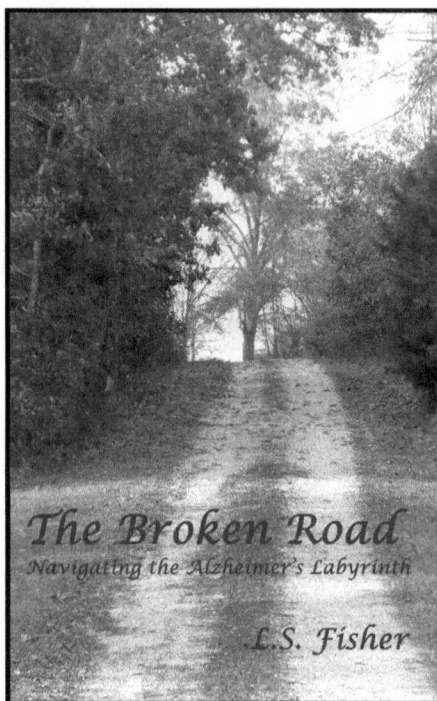

Mozark Press
PO Box 1746
Sedalia, MO 65302

www.MozarkPress.com
www.lsfisher.com

The Heart Remembers
Early Onset Alzheimer's Essays

By L. S. Fisher

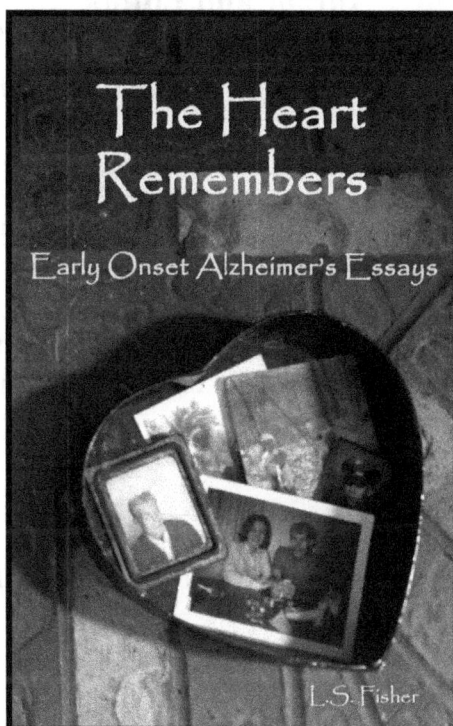

Mozark Press
PO Box 1746
Sedalia, MO 65302

www.MozarkPress.com
www.lsfisher.com

Memory Talk

Linda Fisher
Alzheimer's Speaker

Author and Editor
of
Alzheimer's Anthology of Unconditional Love

Linda is a longtime Alzheimer's Association volunteer and advocate. She speaks from her personal experience as a primary caregiver for her husband who lived with early onset dementia for ten years. She will speak to your group or organization about Alzheimer's or writing life stories. Choose from the following presentations, or request a different Alzheimer's or writing topic:

Writing as Therapy: Rocks and Pebbles

Where are your real life stories? Learn how to reconnect with the pebbles of your life and how writing these stories can be therapeutic. Discover slice-of-life moments that only you know. Suitable for senior adult writing groups, caregivers, and support groups.

Alzheimer's Voices of Experience

Learn about Alzheimer's from short excerpts of the heartfelt stories collected in *Alzheimer's Anthology of Unconditional Love.* These true stories allow you to glimpse the lives of real people who have embarked upon an unwilling journey into the world of dementia. This presentation gives a face and voice to the statistics of a baffling disease. Suitable for nursing home staff, caregivers, Alzheimer's staff and volunteers, civic organizations, and people who want to know more about dementia.

Alzheimer's Can Happen at Any Age

A PowerPoint presentation that focuses on raising awareness that Alzheimer's is a neurological brain disease and not a normal part of aging. Suitable for nursing home staff, caregivers, Alzheimer's staff and volunteers, civic organizations, and people who want to know more about dementia.

Alzheimer's Caregivers: Survive and Thrive

A workshop to develop caregiver coping skills. Linda speaks from her personal experience as a primary caregiver for her husband who lived with early onset dementia for ten years. Suitable for caregivers.

Alzheimer's Caregiver Stress

A PowerPoint presentation covering signs of stress and stress management techniques. Linda learned coping skills from her personal experience as a primary caregiver for her husband. Suitable for caregivers and support groups.

Alzheimer's Communication: Hear their Voices

A presentation to develop communication skills. Linda draws on her experience as the primary caregiver for her husband and his difficulty communicating due to aphasia. Suitable for nursing home staff, caregivers, volunteers, and civic organizations.

Caregiver Emotions

This one-hour seminar will help you identify seven caregiver emotions and develop strategies to cope with the emotional rollercoaster. This presentation focuses on the Alzheimer's caregiver, but care partners of other serious ailments can benefit from this program.

To schedule a presentation:

Email: lfisher@lsfisher.com

From the Author

My therapist is on call twenty-four hours a day. Some of my most successful sessions occur in the middle of the night when I'm comfortable in my pajamas. I grab a pen and paper or fire up my laptop and write through my worries, hurt, or anger.

I began journaling when I was twelve years old, and knew that writing helped me collect my thoughts and look at my problems more objectively. After I married and began to raise a family, I put away my journals except for an occasional travel log.

When my husband Jim developed dementia at forty-nine, I felt the need to write again. Through the ten years of Jim's dementia, I kept a detailed journal, mostly on tape. When I later transcribed the tapes, I re-discovered a wealth of information to help me heal.

Just like talking to a therapist, writing eased me through the emotionally draining decade of Jim's illness. The power of the pen healed my spirit.

Gathering and editing stories for *Alzheimer's Anthology of Unconditional Love* gave me purpose after Jim's death. I'm still working on a memoir and hope these stories can help others along their journeys.

My love of writing complements my volunteer work and helps me focus on the power of positive thinking and action.

L. S. Fisher lives, works, and writes in Sedalia, MO. The greatest tragedy in her life led to her greatest accomplishments. If her husband had not developed dementia, she would have spent her days working and her evenings at home. Instead, she has been recognized locally, statewide, and nationally for her Alzheimer's Association volunteer work.

Website: www.lsfisher.com
Blog: http://earlyonset.blogspot.com

Essay originally published in *Bylines 2010 Writer's Desk Calendar*, Snowflake Press, www.bylinescalendar.com

MoZark Press
Sedalia, Missouri

Mozark Press is a small publishing company in central Missouri dedicated to producing quality paperback books. We will publish short story collections, inspirational works, anthologies, general fiction, and non-fiction.

Mozark Press plans to publish 1-5 new books per year that meet our standards. We expect manuscripts to be polished and error-free when submitted.

Contact us if you want to see your work in print, but haven't been successful with a major publishing company. Maybe you have considered self-publishing, but do not have the time or know-how to do it yourself. We've been there, done that, and wouldn't wish it on anyone.

We are interested in new or established authors. Mozark Press will partner with our authors. We will provide a complimentary author webpage for one year. We won't ask you to sign a long-term contract.

We do not accept unsolicited manuscripts. If you have a completed manuscript, you would like us to consider, send a query letter to:

Publisher@mozarkpress.com